Pathfinder®Guides

L District

Central Lakeland

Walks

Compiled by
Terry Marsh

Text:	Terry Marsh
Photography:	Terry Marsh
Editorial:	Ark Creative (UK) Ltd
Design:	Ark Creative (UK) Ltd

 This product includes mapping data licensed from Ordnance Survey® with the permission of the Controller of Her Majesty's Stationery Office. © Crown Copyright 2009. All rights reserved. Licence number 150002047. Ordnance Survey, the OS symbol and Pathfinder are registered trademarks and Explorer, Landranger and Outdoor Leisure are trademarks of the Ordnance Survey, the national mapping agency of Great Britain.

ISBN 978-1-85458-498-4

While every care has been taken to ensure the accuracy of the route directions, the publishers cannot accept responsibility for errors or omissions, or for changes in details given. The countryside is not static: hedges and fences can be removed, field boundaries can alter, footpaths can be rerouted and changes in ownership can result in the closure or diversion of some concessionary paths. Also, paths that are easy and pleasant for walking in fine conditions may become slippery, muddy and difficult in wet weather, while stepping stones across rivers and streams may become impassable.

If you find an inaccuracy in either the text or maps, please write to Crimson Publishing at the address below.

First published in Great Britain 2009 by Crimson Publishing, a division of:
Crimson Business Ltd,
Westminster House, Kew Road, Richmond, Surrey, TW9 2ND

www.totalwalking.co.uk

Printed in Singapore. 1/09

A catalogue record for this book is available from the British library.

Front cover: Little Langdale Tarn
Previous page: Looking north from the slopes of Wansfell Pike

Contents

Approximate walk times

 Up to 2 hours   2½–3½ hours   4 hours and over

The walk times are provided as a guide only and are calculated using an average walking speed of 2½mph (4km/h), adding one minute for each 10m (33ft) of ascent, and then rounding the result to the nearest half hour.

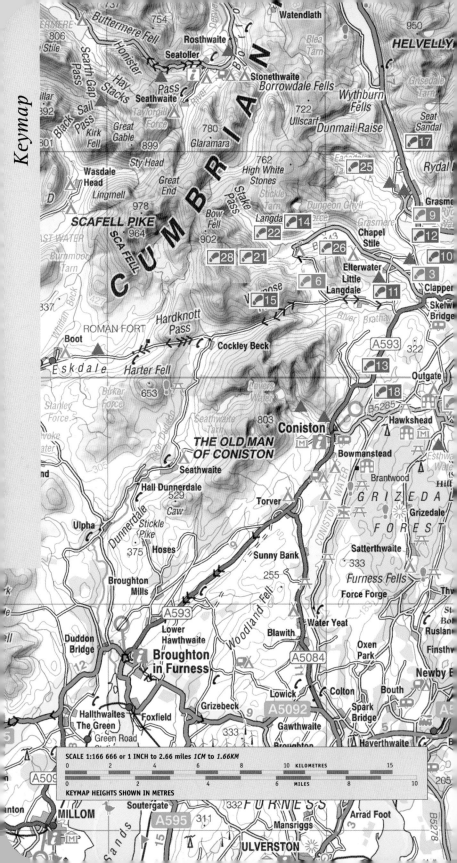

Keymap

SCALE 1:166 666 or 1 INCH to 2.66 miles *1CM* to *1.66KM*

KILOMETRES

MILES

KEYMAP HEIGHTS SHOWN IN METRES

Walk	Page	Start	Nat. Grid Reference	Distance	Time	Height Gain
Bowfell	89	Great Langdale	NY 286061	7½ miles (12km)	4½ hrs	2,855ft (870m)
Bowness Heights and Brant Fell	20	Bowness-on-Windermere	SD 403969	4¼ miles (7km)	2 hrs	590ft (180m)
Claife Heights	59	Windermere (west shore)	SD 388954	6¾ miles (11km)	3½ hrs	1,265ft (385m)
Crinkle Crags	66	Great Langdale	NY 286061	7 miles (11.5km)	4 hrs	2,820ft (860m)
Elterwater	37	Elterwater	NY 328048	5½ miles (8.9km)	2½ hrs	835ft (255m)
Far Easedale and Helm Crag	79	Mill Bridge, Grasmere	NY 336091	8¾ miles (14km)	4½ hrs	2,200ft (670m)
Grey Crag and Alcock Tarn	31	Grasmere	NY 339073	3¾ miles (6km)	2 hrs	1,035ft (315m)
Grisedale Tarn	53	Mill Bridge, Grasmere	NY 336090	5 miles (8km)	3 hrs	1,900ft (580m)
The Langdale valleys	82	Great Langdale	NY 294064	8½ miles (13.5km)	4½ hrs	1,690ft (515m)
Latterbarrow	18	Hawkshead	SD 354980	3¾ miles (6km)	2 hrs	720ft (220m)
Loughrigg Fell	34	Tarn Foot, Loughrigg	NY 346039	4½ miles (7.3km)	2½ hrs	1,395ft (425m)
Loughrigg Tarn and the Brathay	16	Silverthwaite	NY 341037	3 miles (4.6km)	1½ hrs	525ft (160m)
Orrest Head and Allen Knott	28	Windermere	SD 414987	4½ miles (7.2km)	2 hrs	755ft (230m)
Pavey Ark and Harrison Stickle	46	Great Langdale	NY 294064	3¾ miles (6km)	2½ hrs	2,200ft (670m)
Pike o'Blisco and Cold Pike	48	Three Shire Stone, Wrynose	NY 277027	3¾ miles (6km)	2½ hrs	1,675ft (510m)
Pike o'Stickle and Stake Pass	69	Great Langdale	NY 294064	6¼ miles (10km)	4 hrs	2,130ft (650m)
Rydal Water and Grasmere	40	Grasmere	NY 339073	5¼ miles (8.5km)	2½ hrs	720ft (220m)
Scandale	86	Ambleside	NY 377044	8¾ miles (14km)	5 hrs	2,625ft (800m)
School Knott	26	Ings	SD 445987	4 miles (6.5km)	2 hrs	540ft (165m)
Scout Scar and Cunswick Fell	76	Kendal	SD 516922	9 miles (14.5km)	4 hrs	1,100ft (335m)
Side Pike and Lingmoor Fell	23	Blea Tarn	NY 296043	3 miles (4.5km)	2 hrs	1,165ft (355m)
Stockghyll Force	12	Ambleside	NY 377045	1¼ miles (2km)	1 hr	295ft (90m)
Sweden Bridges	14	Ambleside	NY 377045	3 miles (5km)	1½ hrs	755ft (230m)
Tarn Hows	56	Hawkshead	SD 354 980	6 miles (9.5km)	3 hrs	985ft (300m)
Tom Heights and Hodge Close	43	Glen Mary Bridge	SD 322999	5 miles (8km)	2½ hrs	1,180ft (360m)
Troutbeck Valley	72	Troutbeck	NY 412 027	7¾ miles (12.5km)	4 hrs	1,330ft (405m)
Wansfell Pike	63	Ambleside	NY 377045	6 miles (9.5km)	3½ hrs	1,837ft (560m)
Wray Castle and Blelham Tarn	50	Red Nab, High Wray	SD 385995	6 miles (9.7km)	3 hrs	785ft (240m)

Comments

An ascent to the highest summit in Great Langdale, the popular and rewarding Bowfell. A romp to an ancient thoroughfare, concluded by an easy and satisfying walk down one of Lakeland's great valleys.

A superb circuit of the hummocky, wooded countryside above and to the east of Bowness, with an optional extension to take in Brant Fell.

Wander across pleasant farmland to a cluster of idyllic tarns set against superb backdrops. The path leads to the wooded summits of Claife Heights, before a gentle stroll along the shore of Windermere.

One of the 'Classic' walks of Lakeland, circling around half of the headwall of Greater Langdale, and visiting one of the most exciting and entertaining fells.

A simple and agreeable circuit of Elter Water lake, with outstanding views of the Langdale Pikes and a visit to a secluded waterfall, before heading for the most attractive of Lakeland footbridges.

A superb walk that ekes as much as possible out of delectable Easedale and the fine craggy ridge to the north; culminating in Helm Crag, better known (from below) as 'The Lion and the Lamb'.

A steep ascent and a steep descent flank a rewarding sojourn along the banks of an unsuspected tarn, hidden high among the fells above Grasmere.

Set off in search of royal treasure, lost for over a thousand years; or simply enjoy a magical setting by a deep tarn amid lofty fells.

A superb walk around Great and Little Langdale, visiting remote tarns, prehistoric sites and one of the finest ancient packhorse bridges of Lakeland.

A surprisingly wide panorama greets arrival at the summit of Latterbarrow, that and one of the tallest summit cairns in the Lake District. Hawkshead is a welcoming place to explore before or after the walk.

A visit to Loughrigg Tarn precedes an ascent onto its neighbouring fell, followed by a steep descent to the shores of Grasmere and a visit to the Rydal Caves, before a trek back across a wild landscape.

Loughrigg Tarn is easy on the eye and makes a most agreeable destination. Here the visit is extended to spend some time in company of the main river hereabouts, the Brathay.

One of the finest viewpoints in Lakeland, Orrest Head is an easy ascent with a splendid reward; turn the walk into something a bit longer by visiting Allen Knott.

A dramatic and inspiring ascent to a lofty tarn, and craggy summits; wild and rugged scenery and outstanding views that will make the heart race with joy.

An excellent excursion to two fells that are often ignored, although they offer fine views of Langdale and Coniston Fells, and welcome respite from more well-trodden ways, especially during the summer .

A splendid romp across high-level moorland follows a steep and steady climb above Dungeon Ghyll. The effort of the first half of the walk is balanced by the ease of the final walk out through Mickleden.

A popular and hugely agreeable circuit of the heart of Wordsworth country; where he lived, where he died, where he lies buried.

A fine, lofty ridge leading to one of the most exquisite, rarely visited dales of Lakeland. Rough fell country, but pure delight on a warm summer's day.

A splendid opportunity to explore a little-known part of Lakeland's limestone country, and to visit a fine viewpoint overlooking Windermere.

A relaxing exploration of dramatic scars to the west of Kendal, and largely unsuspected by visitors to Lakeland. A splendid introduction to the southern limestone country of the Lake District.

An easy start around a beautiful tarn leads into a rocky experience as you grapple with small but complex Side Pike; then a simple ascent leads up on to Lingmoor Fell.

A brief but delightful stroll to a popular Victorian viewpoint, passing through broad-leaved woodlands and the scene, now long gone, of considerable industry.

Two ancient packhorse bridges are visited in this walk into a remote and tranquil valley that was once a thoroughfare across the fells into Patterdale.

An unfamiliar approach to Tarn Hows, starting in the village where Wordsworth went to school, and making the most of splendid countryside.

An undulating walk in two contrasting halves; one passing through the popular setting of Tarn Hows, the other exploring a little-known area of industrial activity.

Inviting exploration but invariably passed through, Troutbeck is a beautiful and easily explored dale, a conservation area endowed with vernacular architecture and associations with Beatrix Potter.

A justly popular ascent to a marvellous viewpoint, not only of Windermere, but of the fells of Eastern Lakeland, around the Kentmere horseshoe.

A chance to explore the quiet side of Windermere, visit a fairy-tale castle, and the childhood summer residence of Beatrix Potter. Woodlands, tarns and lakeshore combine in a walk of tranquility.

Introduction to the Lake District

Unknown territory

The early visitors to the Lake District ventured here with a measure of fear and excitement, not knowing for certain what to expect. Early explorers – Celia Fiennes, Daniel Defoe, Thomas Pennant, Thomas Gray – all described the landscape in various ways, striking a nice (but probably unintentional) balance between description that was inviting and text that proved a deterrent. We know there were no dragons in the Lake District, nor is it suggested that anyone ever seriously thought there were. But many visitors believed there was mischief and ill-fortune awaiting anyone who ventured too far from the beaten track. Thomas Gray himself, a much- and unfairly maligned travel writer, arguably one of Britain's best, declined to venture all the way down Borrowdale to Seatoller and beyond for fear of what lay there, basing that fear on tales spun by local people. When you recognise that the way down Borrowdale and by way of Styhead into Wasdale is an ancient packhorse route, in use at the time of Gray's visits, and couple that with the certainty that parts of the fells were used for smuggling and illicit whisky distilling, it begs the question that there was a certain amount of codswallop veiling the Lakeland fells.

Yet the dread of mountains persisted for some time, although things were soon to change. John Taylor, the so-called 'Water Poet' (who journeyed on foot from London to Edinburgh and beyond, and described the experience in *Penniless Pilgrimage*), felt the pull of the mountains. And did so at a time when the norm was still to look on mountainous areas with a fearful eye, as did, for example, Daniel Defoe, who described Westmoreland (sic) as being 'a country eminent only for being the wildest, most barren and frightful of any that I have passed over in England, or even in Wales it self; the west side, which borders on Cumberland, is indeed bounded by a chain of almost unpassable mountains, which, in the language of the country, are called Fells.'

In spite of these claims – and there is some doubt that Defoe ever got farther north than Lancaster – people seem to have been climbing Skiddaw, at least, for some centuries. Bishop Nicolson of Carlisle, for example, went up with friends as early as 1684 ... for the mere pleasure of going there, which Ruskin's secretary, W.G. Collingwood notes '... seems to have been a well-known point of view.'

The Victorian era

But quite when the modern cult of walking took off is not certain. The Victorians, keen on exploration and appreciation of the landscape, certainly came to the Lakes in large numbers, especially after the arrival of the railways

Tarn Hows and Black Fell

in the mid-19th century. Captain Joseph Budworth rambled through the Lakes in 1792 and 1795, covering more than 240 miles. Unaffected by the prevailing Romantic mood, he walked freely among the fells and 'trundled boulders down Helvellyn', doing so for the experience and to enjoy himself. What is remarkable about his accounts of walking in the Lake District is the appealing frankness, which caused him to confess his own inadequacy as when he bandaged up one eye before crossing the fell slopes below Langdale Pikes, in order not to see what lay below. Budworth's ascent of the Old Man of Coniston is often cited as the first 'tourist' ascent of the mountain. That was barely 200 years ago, and as we romp the fells today it is difficult to imagine what it might have felt like to have made the first, or, at least, the first recorded, exploration of the fells.

Wordsworth and the so-called Lake Poets are generally credited (or blamed, depending on your point of view), for bringing increasing numbers of tourists to the Lake District. That is neither entirely true nor fair, other writers were here before them. But Wordsworth lived in the Lake District and knew it intimately, and certain it is that his descriptive writings did much to attract visitors. Even so, the vogue for personal narratives masquerading as guidebooks went on well into the 19th century, most written on the basis of brief tours by outsiders. They were significant in creating a literary illusion, leaving little to the individual's imagination, directing their appreciation of the landscape rather than influencing or persuading independent exploration and discovery. What made the work of Wordsworth, Harriet Martineau and William Green so different, and therefore valuable, is that they lived here, and knew the region intimately.

The Lake District today is all things to all men (and women). Each visitor sees the Lakeland landscape in a different way. Some describe the fells, others the dales, the rivers, lakes, tarns and meres. There are many landscape features, but overall, in a physical sense, it is the fells and the lakes that are the key to the region's popularity. And although water appears throughout the length and breadth of Britain, in the Lake District it is the presence of so much water in such a compact area set among dramatic fells and beautiful dales, themselves bounded north, west and south by even greater expanses of water, that makes this region so remarkably different from other parts of Britain, and so palpably unique – the 'Odd Corner of England' as it has been called.

Nor can it be overlooked that the Lake District comprises the only significant mountainous region in England, uniquely distinctive, so much so

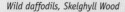
Wild daffodils, Skelghyll Wood

that the National Park Authority was able to adopt as its emblem the arrangement of fells at the head of Wasdale, arguably the most inaccessible dale for the vast majority of visitors. Yet it is a landscape arrangement at once symbolic, iconic and instantly recognisable.

Central Lakeland
No attempt to gather fells into convenient groups can ever be entirely satisfactory. The Lake District does not lend itself to neat division, but in this arrangement of walks, the reader is invited to explore a delectable part of the District that is for the most part comparatively little known, although you will encounter many other discerning walkers who share your vision.

The central south-north thrust of Lakeland is clear enough; it runs from Plumgarth on the outskirts of Kendal, by way of Windermere and Ambleside up to Grasmere. A pedant would insist that it continues farther, north through the valley occupied by Thirlmere, to the outskirts of Keswick. But a line had to be drawn somewhere, and it lay across Dunmail Raise. Reaching westwards from Ambleside runs the valley of Great Langdale, its great headwall of Crinkle Crags and Bowfell providing a perfect complement to the iconic Langdale Pikes. And Great Langdale merely provides an excuse, if one were needed, to venture over into Little Langdale, and by a tenuous link to the wooded farmlands around Hawkshead. Some excursions are made to the east of the central thrust, but only tentatively, as this area falls for the most part in another volume.

Geologically, but in very simple terms that no geologist would find acceptable, the area covered in this book reaches from the limestone country in the south, to the great craggy fells of the Borrowdale Volcanic Series of rocks that so please the ardent rock climbers. It is a dramatic contrast: the limestone provides gently undulating landscapes mottled by hummocky terrain that is a pleasure to explore. The harder rocks present a different challenge, and an altogether dissimilar scene, one of steep cliffs, crag-girt fell summits and myriad rocky ways. This book takes you on an exploration of this marvellous landscape.

This book includes a list of waypoints alongside the description of the walk, so that you can enjoy the full benefits of gps should you wish to. For more information on using your gps, read the *Pathfinder® Guide GPS for Walkers*, by gps teacher and navigation trainer, Clive Thomas (ISBN 978-0-7117-4445-5). For essential information on map reading and basic navigation, read the *Pathfinder® Guide Map Reading Skills* by outdoor writer, Terry Marsh (ISBN 978-0-7117-4978-8). Both titles are available in bookshops or can be ordered online at www.totalwalking.co.uk

Stockghyll Force

		GPS waypoints
Start	Ambleside	 NY 377 045
Distance	1¼ miles (2km)	**A** NY 381 045
Height gain	295 feet (90m)	**B** NY 385 046
Approximate time	1 hour	
Parking	Ambleside	
Route terrain	Road walking; woodland	
Ordnance Survey maps	Landranger 90 (Penrith & Keswick),Explorer OL7 (The English Lakes – South-eastern area)	

Stock Ghyll, a tributary of the River Rothay, rises on the steep fell slopes of Red Screes above the Kirkstone Pass. Just east of Ambleside, it descends through a series of waterfalls and low cascades that was a fashionable, if brief, Victorian excursion; it remains justly popular today.

The walk begins from the centre of Ambleside, at the **Salutation Inn**, itself one of the oldest inns in Lakeland. Locate the minor lane to the east of the Salutation (walk through a passageway between a bank and the old market hall). The lane, signposted for Stock Ghyll and Wansfell, climbs gently round a bend to the edge of Stock Ghyll woodlands. Here, Stock Ghyll is but a broad stream. Yet within strides, you reach a path **A** branching left into the woodlands, and clearly signposted for

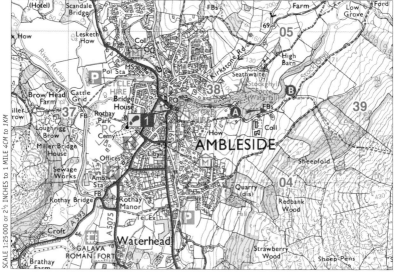

Stockghyll Force.

Stock Ghyll was once of considerable importance to the economic well-being of the people of Ambleside, supporting as it did no less than 12 watermills that were used to generate power needed for the manufacture of bobbins, fabrics, paper and for grinding corn.

In another respect it acquired a tainted notoriety when the Stock Ghyll woodlands, including the falls, were privately acquired, and the owner, having erected fences all around the woodlands, decided to charge for admission. A degree of equanimity was restored only when the town council decided to buy the land for what was the extortionate sum of £4,100. In 1880, more than 20,000 visitors passed into the woodlands to view the falls.

The way to the falls is waymarked with red arrows, and leads you unerringly through this lovely woodland, carpeted in springtime with daffodils. As you walk through the woodland, you will notice a footbridge spanning the ghyll on your left. Ignore this for the moment; you will use it on the return stretch.

For the moment, continue a steady upward climb through the trees to arrive at a couple of viewing platforms on the left. The waterfall here is quite impressive, by no means the greatest, but set in a lovely nook surrounded by ferns and broad-leaved trees.

Continue upwards, above the viewing platforms to a bridge **B** spanning the ghyll. Over this turn left, now descending, and follow the path downwards to the footbridge noticed earlier in the walk. Once across this it is simply a question of retracing steps back to Ambleside. ●

Stockghyll Force

Sweden Bridges

			GPS waypoints
Start	Ambleside market cross		NY 377 045
Distance	3 miles (5km)		Ⓐ NY 378 058
Height gain	755 feet (230m)		Ⓑ NY 379 067
Approximate time	1½ hours		Ⓒ NY 376 057
Parking	Ambleside		
Route terrain	Fell farmland; stony tracks; road walking		
Ordnance Survey maps	Landranger 90 (Penrith & Keswick), Explorer OL7 (The English Lakes –South-eastern area)		

Scandale is a fine, fell-framed valley running north from Ambleside; it is visited more fully in Walk 27, but the present walk gives a preview, a hint of how tranquil a retreat the valley is. Culminating at High Sweden Bridge, the walk is deservedly popular at any time of year. The name 'Sweden' is believed to derive from 'swithen', a reference to land cleared by burning. The two bridges visited in this walk are packhorse bridges, an indication that Scandale and the pass at its head were once used as a through-route to Patterdale.

Start the walk from the market cross in Ambleside, and set off up North Road. This is the oldest part of the town, known as Ambleside above Stock, and it is here that the town developed as industry grew. Later, after the railway came to Windermere in 1847, tourists came to stay, brought here on stagecoaches operated by the Rigg family who then managed the Windermere Hotel.

When you reach the top of Smithy Brow, near the **Golden Rule inn**, keep forward into Kirkstone Road, and shortly turn left into Sweden Bridge Lane. Keep going up the lane, which becomes increasingly narrow and leads to a gate giving onto an enclosed track. The track climbs steadily between walls, and when it forks, at a gate, bear left.

The track wanders

High Sweden Bridge

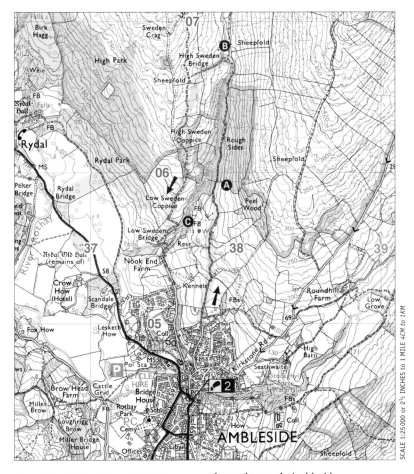

SCALE 1:25000 or 2½ INCHES to 1 MILE 4CM to 1KM

0	200	400	600	800 METRES	1
					KILOMETRES
					MILES
0	200	400	600 YARDS	½	

upwards at a gentle gradient, with numerous fine views of the Fairfield Horseshoe, and eventually leads into an area of mixed woodland **A**. The ascending track finally breaks free of the woodland and just a short way farther you need to bear left, leaving the Scandale valley track as it reaches High Sweden Bridge **B**.

Cross the bridge and, through the gate on the other side, turn left and follow an ascending path that soon climbs beside a wall to a ladder-stile. After the stile, the path leads off to the left to locate a gap in a wall beyond which a broad grassy track starts to descend towards Ambleside.

The track scampers delightfully down the southern end of the Low Pike ridge towards Ambleside, with views down the length of Windermere. Eventually the path curves round to a gate at a wall corner **C**. Now it continues the descent with good views to the right of the Langdale Pikes, Bowfell, Crinkle Crags and the Coniston Fells.

The track soon makes a loop to cross Low Sweden Bridge. Walk up to Nook End Farm and pass through the farmyard. Beyond, now simply follow a surfaced lane (Nook Lane), back to Ambleside. At the end of Nook Lane, turn right and walk down to the main road and there turn left, following the road to complete the walk. ●

Loughrigg Tarn and the Brathay

Start	Silverthwaite	**GPS waypoints**	
Distance	3 miles (4.6km)	🖉 NY 341 037	
Height gain	525 feet (160m)	Ⓐ NY 341 042	
		Ⓑ NY 345 046	
Approximate time	1½ hours	Ⓒ NY 346 040	
Parking	At start	Ⓓ NY 343 035	
Route terrain	Narrow paths through bracken; rough tracks; country lanes		
Ordnance Survey maps	Landranger 90 (Penrith & Keswick), Explorer OL7 (The English Lakes – South-eastern area)		

Loughrigg Tarn sits like a jewel in a neat hollow below Loughrigg Fell. Its circuit, which is quite delightful, can be made easily by driving up to Tarn Foot, but here the walk is extended to include a stroll along the River Brathay and a visit to Skelwith Force.

🖉 Locate the narrow path at the western end of the car park and follow this up alongside the garden wall of Silverthwaite Cottage, climbing steeply at first, but with lovely views of the Langdale Pikes to enliven the way. At a cross-path, keep forward along an obvious route across the shoulder of Little Loughrigg to arrive at a cottage (Crag Head) Ⓐ, and here gain your first view of Loughrigg Tarn.

Loughrigg Tarn was a favoured place of Wordsworth, who, in his *Epistle to Sir George Howland Beaumont Bart,* likened it to 'Diana's Looking-glass ... round clear and bright as heaven', a reference to Lake Nemi, the mirror of Diana in Rome.

Descend to the left of the cottage, and then immediately bear left onto a vehicle access track that leads out to a surfaced lane. Turn left and walk along the road for 175 yds, and then leave it at a signpost by entering a sloping

pasture on the right. Head down field on a grassy path to a stile, and beyond this go forward, taking the higher of two green paths to a gate giving onto a rough track Ⓑ.

Go through the gate and turn right to follow the track to a gate beside a cottage. Press on, and when the ongoing track forks, branch right, past Dillygarth Cottage and soon reach a surfaced lane. Turn left, descending to a road junction, and there turn right, soon crossing a stream near another road junction Ⓒ.

Bear right and follow the road until, near the top of a rise, you can leave it by turning left onto the rough track (now signposted to Skelwith Bridge) to Crag Head used in the earlier part of the walk.

At Crag Head keep forward, following a path through bracken-clad hummocks dotted with low outcrops until you reach a gate giving into the larch woodland of Neaum Crag. Now a gravel path leads forward to the edge of a holiday park of wooden chalets.

Go forward, descending the service road, following a route waymarked by yellow arrows. At a junction, go forward again but immediately after a sleeping policeman across the road, keep to the right of a chalet called 'Angle Tarn'. Pass another – 'Yew Tree Tarn' – and head for a waymarked path enclosed by a low fence. The path leads to a gate. Go left on a path sandwiched between a wall and a fence, which eventually gives into an open field. Keep forward, descending, and head for a kissing-gate giving on to the main road **D**.

Through the gate, turn left and cross the road, turning right at the nearby junction. Very soon, just before Skelwith Bridge, turn right again, now alongside the River Brathay, heading for the Kirkstone Galleries. At the entrance to the galleries, bear right and walk past the workshops and onto a riverside path beyond.

The Brathay is quite a river. If you trace its line back westwards it will lead to a source close by the Three Shire Stone on Wrynose Pass. On its journey,

it first encounters Little Langdale Tarn, quite a gem in itself, has a few flashy flurries in the shape of Colwith Force before changing direction and heading north to feed into Elter Water, where it joins forces with Great Langdale Beck. Flowing east, the river then has another attempt at waterfalls in the shape of Skelwith Force, but this modest descent simply speeds the river up rather than shows off. Even so, it can be quite exciting when in spate, and *not a place to let children loose.*

Pass Skelwith Force, and walk on to a gate giving into a large and flat pasture. Stick to the main path, which courts the river and gradually circles round to draw level with a small knoll crowned by a stand of trees. Leave the main path here by turning right onto a narrow path passing to the right of the knoll, and continuing to a gate giving into woodland.

A gravel path now leads up through trees to the valley road, emerging from cover at a tricky crossing point directly opposite the Silverthwaite car park. *Take care crossing the road.*

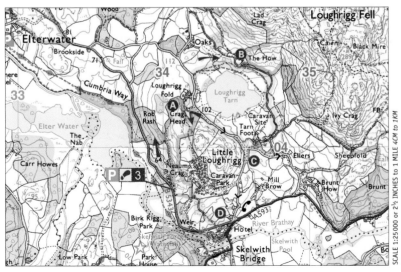

Latterbarrow

		GPS waypoints
Start	Hawkshead	🥾 SD 354 980
Distance	3¾ miles (6km)	Ⓐ SD 359 986
Height gain	720 feet (220m)	Ⓑ SD 371 985
Approximate time	2 hours	Ⓒ SD 362 992
Parking	Hawkshead (Pay and Display)	
Route terrain	Woodland trails; some road walking; exposed fell summit	
Ordnance Survey maps	Landranger 97 (Kendal & Morecambe), Explorer OL7 (The English Lakes – South-eastern area)	

The view from the top of Latterbarrow makes the ascent of this comparatively low fell disproportionately rewarding, and one of the most popular walks from Hawkshead. Storm damage and tree felling has merely added to the fell's appeal as a vantage point.

🥾 Hawkshead is an immensely fashionable place to visit, especially by those following the Wordsworth trail. But leave your exploration of the village for another time, or the end of the walk, and set off from the main car park by leaving via the vehicular entrance and turning right to a T-junction. Here, go left onto the Sawrey road, and at the first junction, bear left along a narrow, vergeless lane that leads to the hamlet of Colthouse.

Colthouse, was one of the remote Lakeland communities visited by George Fox, who in 1653, projected the hamlet into the Quaker limelight. It still has a Friends' Meeting House. The hamlet is also one of the places Wordsworth lodged during his school days in Hawkshead.

Walk through the hamlet, and continue north along the road for about 275 yds until, beyond the last of the buildings, you can leave the road by turning sharply to the right, opposite the entrance to Gill Bank Ⓐ, and pass through a gate onto a rising stony track. After a few strides, where the track forks, bear right.

The continuing track climbs steadily throughout as it crosses the wooded landscape between Latterbarrow and Colthouse Heights, although it soon becomes clear that a great swathe of the fell has been storm damaged and/or cleared of trees. Ignore any branching paths and head in a direction roughly north of east to reach a wall corner Ⓑ.

Go through a gate and along a stony track at a woodland boundary to a wall

Summit cairn on Latterbarrow

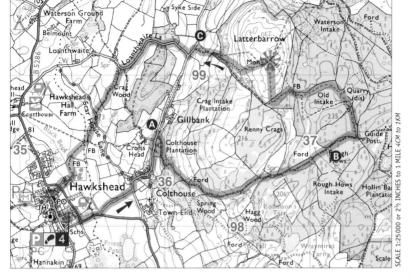

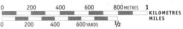

SCALE 1:25000 or 2½ INCHES to 1 MILE 4CM to 1KM

gap with a signpost nearby. Here, turn left, taking to a clear path across a cleared area. Across this, a stepped path leads up to another gap in a wall, through which you turn right beside the wall. Shortly, swing left, again crossing cleared ground and following a path that takes you back into forest. A clear path now leads along the forest boundary to a step-stile in a corner.

Once across the stile, turn right to climb onto the top of Latterbarrow, easing upwards on a clear track that leads directly to the enormous cairn that pinpoints the summit.

From the top of the fell, take a direct line along a grassy path, targeting the village of Hawkshead to the south west. Lower down, the path joins another and leads steadily downwards to intercept a country lane **C**. Turn left along the lane for about 50 yds, and then go right into Loanthwaite Lane.

After about 750 yds, near farm buildings, take the second of two signposted paths on the left (for Hawkshead), and use this to follow a surfaced route across meadows to Scar House Lane, which is little more than an enclosed rough track.

Turn left along the track, but very soon go right, into another meadow, across which the continuing path leads back to Hawkshead. At the first of the cottages on entering the village, turn right over a footbridge and walk along an enclosed path that eventually emerges onto a main road. The starting car park is off to your left at this point, but for a safer route cross the road, continuing ahead on cobbles past some fine old cottages and through an archway to emerge at the rear of the **Kings Arms Hotel**. Turn left and follow the road out of the village until you reach the turning into the car park.

Hawkshead is a village that developed at the junction of packhorse trails used to link the Windermere ferry with the Coniston valley. Wordsworth attended school here from the age of nine until 1787, and the village has close associations with Beatrix Potter, who lived not far away at Near Sawrey. Her husband, solicitor William Heelis, had his office in Hawkshead; it is now the Beatrix Potter Gallery. ●

Bowness Heights and Brant Fell

		GPS waypoints
Start	Bowness-on-Windermere	📖 SD 403 969
Distance	3¾ miles (6km), plus 0.6 mile (1km) for Brant Fell	🅐 SD 413 970
Height gain	590 feet (180m), plus 195 feet (60m) for Brant Fell	🅑 SD 420 976 🅒 SD 423 971
Approximate time	1¾ hours, 2 hours including to Brant Fell	🅓 SD 423 962 🅔 SD 408 966
Parking	Bowness-on-Windermere	
Route terrain	Farmland; woodland; rough fell ground	
Ordnance Survey maps	Landranger 97 (Kendal & Morecambe), Explorer OL7 (The English Lakes – South-eastern area)	

The name Bowness Heights is the author's invention, and refers to that lovely hummocky, woody, amorphous wedge of ground that lies above and to the east of Bowness-on-Windermere, and through which the Dales Way completes (or starts) its journey.

The walk begins from anywhere near the lakeshore and sets off up the road as if heading for Windermere, but soon you branch right into Helm Road. Bowness-on-Windermere is arguably the Lake District's most popular tourist destination, but was a busy place long before tourism. Its church dates from the 15th century and probably earlier,

On Bowness Heights

and there are records of inns here in the 16th century, a sure sign of commercial activity. The lake has been a highway for centuries, but today the architectural heritage is largely Victorian and Edwardian, built by wealthy business-men from the Lancashire mill towns.

The curious visitor will find especial delight in the narrow streets of Lowside behind the church, which are characteristic of the town, then a lakeside village, long before the railway arrived at what is today Windermere.

📖 Climb steeply and soon pass the **Windermere Hydro Hotel**, which was built in the late 19th century in response to the vogue for water cure treatments that prevailed. At a road junction you can briefly divert left to the Biskey Howe viewpoint, but then return to the same spot, and continue in the original direction along a path for Post Knott and Helm Farm.

A short way farther on, continue along the path for 'The Helm'. At the next junction, where the lane divides, take the middle one of three options, still signposted for Helm Farm. When the ongoing lane forks again, bear right, and when it swings sharply to the right 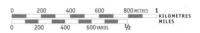, leave it by turning left at a kissing-gate (redundant) to follow a waymarked path with a fence on the right. The path leads to another gate beyond which it runs out to a gap stile, after which the path bears right around the rear of a housing estate.

At a signpost, turn obliquely right, steeply ascending through a small broad-leaved woodland, and following a route for School Knott. A kissing-gate at the gable of a house gives onto a path that passes Low Lickbarrow Farm and Lickbarrow Cottage, beyond which you reach the edge of a large pasture.

Keep forward, and then bear right to a kissing-gate giving on to a lane.

Cross to the through-stile nearby, and then take the path for Old Droomer, which now goes forward beside a wall. When the wall changes direction, keep forward, descending across a field to a low ladder-stile beyond which you cross a stream and then ascend steps to meet a broad track ⓑ. Turn right. The designation of this track as a Byway Open to All Traffic (a BOAT) is an indication of its longevity as a thoroughfare.

As the lane, which is walled, bends to the right, leave it by going forward through a gate onto a continuing path, free of walls. At a gate the track enters light woodland from which it soon escapes and continues as a delightful track across the western slopes of School Knott.

At a waymark ⓒ the track forks. Bear right having now joined the Dales

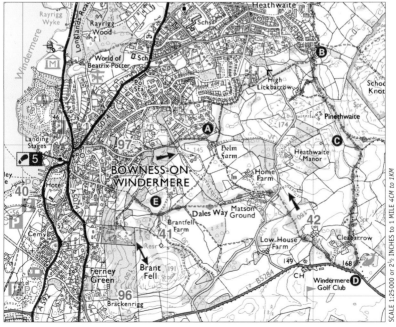

Looking down on Bowness

Way which will guide you all the way back to Bowness. The ongoing track is quite delightful, and at Parrock Cross becomes surfaced, leading out to meet the B5284 **D**.

Just before joining the road, clamber over a stile on the right to gain a path away from the road. When this re-emerges at the roadside, turn right onto the lane for Low Cleabarrow.

Just before the cottages and farm at Low Cleabarrow, leave the track by branching left through a gate onto a signposted path for Bowness and Matson Ground. After the gate, turn right to follow a wall down field, at the bottom of which you pass through three gates in quick succession before walking up to a waymark nearby. The route now crosses a wooded knoll before descending to a wall/gate. Cross the next field to a gate giving onto a road. Press on through the gate opposite to follow an enclosed path that leads down to Matson Ground Farm. Go through a narrow gate opposite and then another to pursue a path alongside a small tarn.

The path passes through a wall/gate and reaches a narrow lane beyond. Turn right for a few strides, but then leave the lane by branching left to a metal gate giving into a large, hummocky pasture. Strike across the pasture on a clear route to a gate in the far corner.

Bear left alongside another wall, and then walk out to meet a lane, north of Brantfell Farm. Keep on in the same direction, along a wall-enclosed track to reach a gate **E**.

(Walkers who wish to visit the summit of Brant Fell should turn left here, up a few steps into a sloping field. Bear a little to the right, but keep an eye open for a waymark among the trees on your left. Climb steeply to pass this to a through-stile in a concealed wall corner. Over the stile, go left beside a fence, but when this changes direction, head down through a dip, and up through the rocky outcrops that adorn the top of Brant Fell. Retrace your steps to the gate **E**.)

Bear right alongside a wall. The path descends to intercept a broad track. Cross the track and continue descending towards the edge of Bowness. The path leads down to a gate at the top of a road, which is now simply followed back into town. ●

Side Pike and Lingmoor Fell

		GPS waypoints	
Start	Blea Tarn	📷	NY 296 043
Distance	3 miles (4.5km)	🅐	NY 289 051
Height gain	1,165 feet (355m)	🅑	NY 294 053
Approximate time	2 hours	🅒	NY 303 046
Parking	National Trust car park, Blea Tarn (Pay and Display)		
Route terrain	Rough fell country; crags and a steep descent		
Ordnance Survey maps	Landranger 90 (Penrith & Keswick), Explorer OL6 (The English Lakes – South-western area)		

For many visitors, Blea Tarn set against the backdrop of Pike o'Blisco on the one hand and Lingmoor Fell on the other, is a perfect vision of Lakeland. That it rests in a little hanging valley between the two Langdale valleys, and is approachable only along narrow, twisting and bumpy roads makes it all the more appealing. Walk 26 will be seen to visit the tarn on a great circuit of the valleys, but in this walk, the tarn is the starting point for a short but potentially very exciting trip onto Lingmoor Fell and the lower, but more problematic, Side Pike to the north.

📷 On leaving the car park, cross the road and walk down the gravel path opposite that leads around the southern edge of the tarn. Go through a gate and, on crossing a footbridge spanning the outflow from the tarn, turn immediately right along a continuing path that runs up the west side of the tarn, and leaves the National Trust grounds at another gate farther on.

Now simply follow a clear and broad track northwards until you arrive at the road, near a cattle-grid 🅐.

While walking along this stretch you can apply your mind to a problem that looms ahead. This walk visits the top of Side Pike, but you can see that its right-hand edge is vertical. Getting around this impediment involves some nifty footwork on narrow paths on rock ledges; this is likely to be an issue for

anyone who suffers from vertigo, but is otherwise little more than a call for caution in the placement of feet. There is also a very tight passageway between rocks through which you will have to squeeze (see later). Thankfully, *there is an alternative path skirting the bottom of Side Pike, which avoids all these difficulties, rising by a fence across a brackeny slope to meet the original line below the vertical cliffs.* You need to think now which way you want to go. The former is typical of the kind of situation you find in the Lake District – there is another tight squeeze on Scafell, for example; the latter is a way round it, a compromise, but one that does not visit the summit of Side Pike.

Cross the road and a ladder-stile to be faced with four radiating paths. That on the right leads to the low-level variant path, which simply loops around Side Pike before climbing beside a fence to meet a wall **B**, where the main line is rejoined.

Take the second path from the left, rising obliquely half-left across the fell slope. On the ascent there is ample opportunity to stop to admire the constantly improving views. The path casts about as it finds a way through the rocky defences of Side Pike, but leads eventually up to the neat summit marked by a large cairn. Space is at a premium here, so try not to leap for joy too enthusiastically.

For the geologically minded, Side Pike is something of a rarity in the ancient geological record in that it exhibits the three main categories of pyroclastic rock: fallout, surge and flow deposits. Moreover, the rocks found here helped scientists to determine the non-marine nature of the principal rocks, those of the Borrowdale Volcanic Series.

Continuing the walk is what will now occupy your thoughts. The direct route is impossible, as vertical and over-hanging cliffs bar your way. The easiest way is to backtrack towards Side Pike's slightly lower west summit, to locate a clear path that passes to the south of the main summit. You can also reach this by following indistinct paths from the summit, first south and then west, although *you will need to take great care at every step of the way,* and retrace your steps to try another line if you are confronted with anything you are not happy about tackling. Once the path is safely underfoot, you can follow it eastwards. It closes in on those vertical cliffs and shortly presents you with a tight-fitting problem.

Known affectionately as 'Fat Man's Agony', the path squeezes (literally) through a narrow gap (about a foot wide) between the cliff face and a small rock slab. You will need to remove your rucksack and push it ahead of you in order to get through, somewhat indecorously; anyone who fails this test should have taken the diversion from the roadside below. *There is no way*

Blea Tarn and Side Pike

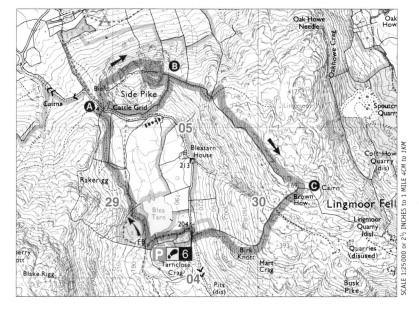

SCALE 1:25000 or 2½ INCHES to 1 MILE 4CM to 1KM

```
0    200   400   600   800 METRES  1
                                      KILOMETRES
                                      MILES
0    200   400   600 YARDS    ½
```

round, and no attempt should be made to pass to the right of the rock slab. If in doubt, go back.

Once through the squeeze, which is nothing like so bad as it seems in print and is done regularly by walkers of all shapes and sizes (with varying degrees

of comfort), the path rises a little more before dropping to a step-stile over a fence, where the valley route joins from the right.

Now continue on easier ground with a wall on your left, as you start the ascent of Lingmoor Fell. The path leads up to a wall corner, where you cross a step-stile in an adjacent fence, and then take an ascending path diagonally on the right, which soon doubles back to run beside a wall.

By sticking with the wall/fence, you are guided unerringly up to the summit of Lingmoor Fell **C**, marked by a large cairn.

Here, cross a simple step-stile on the right to begin the return to the Blea Tarn car park. Stay alongside a fence and wall throughout the descent, although at one point the path moves away from the wall for a while.

When you reach an area of scattered juniper bushes close by a stream, bear right again to cross back towards the wall besides which a path leads down to the road, reaching it just to the south of the car park. Cross the cattle-grid to return to the start. ●

School Knott

Start	Ings	GPS waypoints
Distance	4 miles (6.5km)	🖊 SD 445 987
Height gain	540 feet (165m)	Ⓐ SD 440 980
Approximate time	2 hours	Ⓑ SD 423 976
Parking	Ings (western end of village road)	Ⓒ SD 425 971
Route terrain	Farmland; woodland; rock outcrops; some road walking	Ⓓ SD 436 972
Ordnance Survey maps	Landranger 97 (Kendal & Morecambe), Explorer OL7 (The English Lakes – South-eastern area)	

Invariably passed by as visitors hasten to the shores of Windermere, the limestone country to the south of the A591 offers superb wandering, as those who have tackled the Dales Way will attest. There is a tranquility about the area, a hummocky landscape, small copses and far-reaching views for all the area's modest elevation. Gentle on the eye, gentle on the feet, gentle on the soul.

🖊 Take the quiet, gated lane opposite the small parking area at the start, and follow it as it passes beneath the railway line and makes a wide sweep to the right. Follow the lane (for just under ¹⁄₂ mile) in total and then leave it at a bridleway sign, where the wall on the right bears away from the road Ⓐ. Take care not to leave the road at an earlier footpath.

The bridleway, an old cart track, leads to a gate giving into a small broad-leaved woodland which in spring is carpeted with wood sorrel. Wood sorrel is an ancient woodland indicator species, one of a number of woodland vascular plants that are used, along with other evidence, to indicate the longevity of mature woodlands.

You leave the woodland at another gate, continuing ahead roughly parallel with a wall, to reach Whasdike Farm and a surfaced lane. Turn left along the lane, which soon divides. When it does take the right branch, going forward to a gate. Immediately after the gate, you leave the lane by walking ahead to pass a tin-roofed building, beyond which, you head for a waymark on a small rise. From that, the ongoing path guides you into Schoolknott Plantation.

Take the right-hand one of two paths into the plantation, walking pleasantly through an area of new tree planting to an exit point at another gate. Now keep on in the same direction, ignoring branching paths and tracks, although it is perfectly feasible to bear left and walk up to School Knott at any time. But, to draw the walk out a little longer, keep on to reach a point where, at a gate on the right, a path enters from the direction of Bowness Ⓑ. Now turn left (south-east) and follow a grassy path up onto the knobbly summit of School Knott. The route is anything but precise, nor does it need to be; there is pleasure in visiting each of the minor bumps that adorn the top of the fell. The highest point is rather bald and unadorned. From it you head for a gate close by Scholl Knott Tarn which lies off to the south-east.

Take a path to the right of the tarn, and then walk away from the tarn on a path parallel with an out-flowing stream until you reach a gate on the left beside two ancient larch trees. Turn through the gate, here joining the Dales Way **C**. Ignore the prominent vehicle field track going off to the right, and instead ascend grassy slopes to a way-mark on the skyline. Beyond, you walk to another waymark beside a collapsed wall, and here bear right, teasing a way through low rocky outcrops before swinging left to a gate/wall.

The ongoing path is straightforward and leads to Hag End Farm. The route through the farmyard is waymarked, after which you leave along its access track to intercept a surfaced lane. Turn left here, and shortly after a gate across the lane, branch left (untracked) onto a signposted footpath **D** to a stile/fence, over which you bear right beside the fence on a clear path that leads round to a gated through-stile in a short section of wall.

Over this, walk out to meet another lane. Cross to a kissing-gate opposite, and then follow a grassy path (for Ings) to the group of buildings at Yews. Here, cross a lane by stiles, and bear right through another kissing-gate. After the gate the route is not plainly obvious, but keeps to the right of a row of trees, and generally leads down to another gate towards the bottom left-hand corner of a rough pasture.

Through the gate, continue descending, aiming for a waymark in the middle of the next pasture. The onward route is now waymarked and finally leads out to meet the lane used earlier in the walk. All that remains is to turn left and follow the lane back to Ings. ●

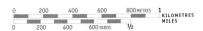

Orrest Head
and Allen Knott

		GPS waypoints
Start	Windermere	🖉 SD 414 987
Distance	4½ miles (7.2km)	Ⓐ NY 418 001
Height gain	755 feet (230m)	Ⓑ NY 414 013
Approximate time	2 hours	Ⓒ NY 411 000
Parking	Lay-by near Windermere Hotel, on A591	
Route terrain	Woodland; farmland	
Ordnance Survey maps	Landrangers 90 (Penrith & Keswick) and 97 (Kendal & Morecambe), Explorer OL7 (The English Lakes – South-eastern area)	

In spite of modest elevation, Orrest Head proves to be a truly fine viewpoint; that it is within the reach of all walkers is a bonus and it is a fair bet that its ascent has inspired many to go on and explore the Lakeland fells more widely.

🖉 You leave the main road directly opposite the National Westminster Bank by taking to a signposted path (a surfaced lane) for Orrest Head. The narrow lane climbs steeply for a while through mixed woodland, teasing a way ever upward. When the tarmac ends, keep forward to walk along a rough track.

When the track forks at a bench, branch right, and where the track later swings right to run beside a wall, turn with it onto a gently rising path beside the wall. An enclosed path leads to a kissing-gate, beyond which a stepped track finishes with a brief flourish onto the summit of Orrest Head.

Ambleside resident, writer, campaigner, radical and atheist, Harriet Martineau, whose *Guide to the Lakes* did much to encourage the first waves of visitors to Lakeland, comments that the top of Orrest Head, unlikely as it may seem, used to be the residence of one Josiah Brown, 'who amused himself ... with welcoming beggars, whom he supplied with meat and lodgings.'

The view is quite special, embracing the fells of Kentmere in one direction and those beyond Windermere –

Windermere from Orrest Head

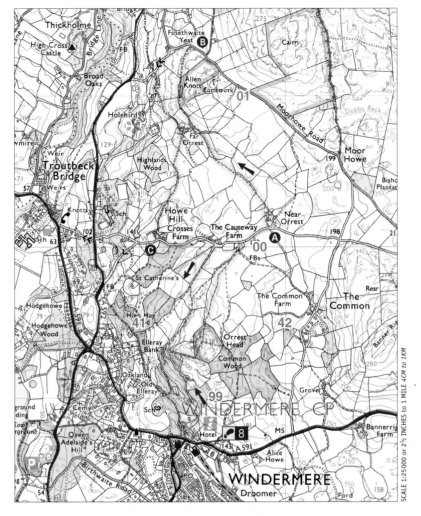

SCALE 1:25000 or 2½ INCHES to 1 MILE 4CM to 1KM

```
0      200    400    600    800 METRES   1
                                         KILOMETRES
                                         MILES
0      200    400    600 YARDS   ½
```

the Langdale and Coniston Fells – in the other. If you are satisfied with that – and well you might be – simply retrace your steps to Windermere.

To extend the walk a little farther, from the top of the fell set off roughly northwards, targeting a conspicuous group of farm buildings close by a small tarn below. A grassy path drops to a through-stile in a wall corner beside a gate and continues descending, crossing a sloping field before running beside a wall and striking across a field punctuated by low rock outcrops, eventually to reach a back lane.

Go right, but about 200 yds farther on leave the road at a through-stile onto a path (signposted to Far Orrest) **A**. Keep to the right-hand field edge to a kissing-gate, cross a brief enclosure to another gate, beyond which lies a small copse. The path now gives into a large pasture. Strike forward to a wall corner, where a stile gives access to the next field. Follow the right-hand field margin, heading for a distant ladder-stile, and passing a lovely pollarded ash tree on the way.

Once over the stile, cross the ensuing

field in a direction half-right and aiming for distant farm buildings. After another ladder-stile, continue towards the farm buildings, following a vehicle track that leads to a kissing-gate. Go through this and another nearby, then turn left along a field edge, passing the farm buildings and then turning through another gate giving onto a walled track.

Bear right and walk along the track, and at its end keep forward beside a wall across the base of high ground, Allen Knott, on the right.

The ongoing path leads to a gate at a wall corner. Through this keep forward, climbing gently on a grassy track before descending to a surfaced lane **B**. On reaching the lane, turn left, taking care against approaching traffic. When the lane forks, branch left and descend to a signposted access for Far Orrest Farm, on the left.

Go onto the access lane, cross a cattle-grid and, when the lane forks, branch left and continue up to Far Orrest Farm. Keep left in front of the buildings to a couple of wide gates. Cross a step-stile on the right (signposted 'Windermere via Crosses') and a farm compound, and then walk out through a gate and along a vehicle track across two fields.

In the second field, the track runs beside a wall, but when it swings left, leave it at a stile and gate in a wall corner. Climb beside a wall, soon reaching more level ground. After a stile/gate, continue on the track beyond eventually emerging at cottages and going forward to a lane **C**.

Turn left and pass Crosses Cottage, and follow the lane to the next farm (Causeway). Opposite the farm entrance, turn right, through a gate and onto a walled track. When the track enters an open field, keep forward beside a wall.

As the on-going track moves away from the wall, stay with it, climbing to a distant stile/gate. Over this, keep right alongside a wall, continuing on a terraced green path with lovely views. The path soon descends to a through-stile beside a gate, and gives into woodland. Almost immediately bear right on a descending track. When the track forks, bear right between walls. At a path T-junction, turn left alongside a high wall.

The descending path finally emerges on the Orrest Head road, a short distance from the main road (A591) and the starting point. ●

Troutbeck from Orrest Head

Grey Crag and Alcock Tarn

		GPS waypoints	
Start	Grasmere		NY 339 073
Distance	3¾ miles (6km)	**A**	NY 344 068
Height gain	1,035 feet (315m)	**B**	NY 348 077
Approximate time	2 hours	**C**	NY 346 084
Parking	Stock Lane car park (Pay and Display)		
Route terrain	Rough fell paths; steep ascent and descent; some road walking		
Ordnance Survey maps	Landranger 90 (Penrith and Keswick), Explorer OL7 (The English Lakes – South-eastern area)		

Grey Crag and sequestered Alcock Tarn prove that it is not only the highest fells and lakes that provide great views and a sense of mountain isolation. On one day a year, however, that peace and quiet is shattered as the Grasmere Sports send fell-runners and hounds up here. But for the rest of the year, peace reigns, and you can enjoy the companionship of solitude and the sounds of silence, for a while, at least.

Set off from the Stock Lane car park, turning left and walking out to the main valley road at Town End. Cross with care and walk into the narrow road opposite that soon passes Dove Cottage *(see Walk 12 for information about Dove Cottage).*

Continue up the lane, ascending easily as far as a branching path on the left **A** next to a coffin stone at the western end of a corpse road that ran, in this instance, from Ambleside to St Oswald's Church in Grasmere *(Walk 12 also provides information about corpse roads).* Leave the road here, by turning left and, keeping to the right of cottages, you soon join a path climbing gently through trees to a bench. Here turn left, taking the signposted route for Alcock Tarn.

Shortly, on reaching Wood Close, the track forks. Bear left into Brackenfell Woodland. The path climbs steadily

through oak and larch. Pass a small pond, and keep climbing. Mercifully, the track zigzags, otherwise this would be a thankless grind. As it is, it offers many opportunities to view the surrounding fells, and there are a number of strategically placed benches at which to recover.

Finally, you pass through a gate in a well-constructed wall into the National Trust's Alcock Tarn reserve. As you climb, so you cross a neat, small stone bridge over the beck issuing from unseen Alcock Tarn, directly below the knobbly point of Grey Crag. Continue following the path up onto Grey Crag **B**, and then walk across to a gap in a nearby wall. Just beyond, Alcock Tarn eases into view.

Alcock Tarn sits on a shelf below Heron Pike, and has been described by one curmudgeon as 'a dreary sheet of

Wordsworth graves, Grasmere

water'. Not even on a misty day is the tarn worthy of such a description. There is a fine sense of isolation about its setting, and by its shores you can be anywhere in the Lake District, far from the brouhaha of the busy valleys.

Originally the tarn was known as Buttercrag Tarn, but the name was changed when a Mr Alcock, who lived at The Hollins in the valley, enlarged the tarn and stocked it with fish.

Keep the tarn to your right, and follow a clear shoreline path that leads to a gate. Beyond lies a remnant tarn, and above this the shapely Butter Crag. Follow the path past this, but spare a thought for the hardy fellrunners who each Grasmere Sports Day (in August), race from the valley to Butter Crag and back.

The so-called Guides Race of the Grasmere Sports was established in Victorian times as a showcase for the courage and strength of the Lake District guides, enabling them to compete for prestige and money. While contemplating how long your ascent took, you might like to reflect on the fact that the winner of the race in 2008 beat the long-standing record, reducing the time for the ascent and descent to a mere 12 minutes 38.5 seconds! In that race, even the last finisher completed the course in a few seconds over 33 minutes.

As you pass below Butter Crag you begin the descent back to the valley. Shortly after starting the descent, you are confronted by a rocky topknot. Keep to the right of this. The path thereafter takes a clear but steep line, diverting to the right around a plantation towards Greenhead Gill.

On reaching the ravine above the gill **C**, the track turns a corner and descends along the plantation boundary and shortly leads down right to the water's edge, being deflected left alongside a moss-covered wall. Walk down to a footbridge, immediately after which you should turn left through a gate onto the head of a surfaced lane.

At a T-junction, go left and walk down to reach the valley road near the **Swan Hotel**. Turn left and cross the road, walking as far as a signposted and enclosed path to Grasmere village on the right. Walk down towards the village, and follow the path to meet the main road (Broadgate). Turn left over a river bridge and walk towards the village centre, but shortly turn left into the Broadgate car park.

Go through the car park to locate a footbridge at the rear giving on to a riverside path that follows the river, crossing it again to walk along its true right bank, but ignoring the Millennium Bridge, opting instead to stay with the path, which curves round to reach the village centre, close by the church.

Turn left here and walk to the Gingerbread Shop, which in Wordsworth's day was the village school, at which both he and his sister taught. Now you can either stay on the road and follow it past the church, or turn into the church grounds to visit the graves of the Wordsworth family. Either way, when you finally pass the church,

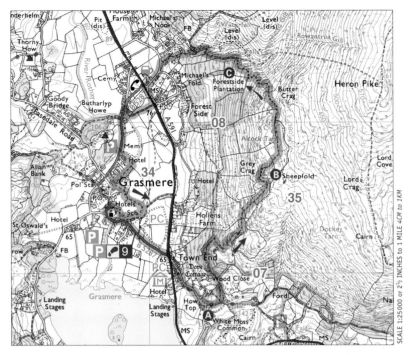

stay along the main round and walk out of Grasmere to return to the car park at the start of the walk.

Grasmere church is dedicated to St Oswald, a 7th-century Christian king of Northumberland. Architecturally, the building is of fascinating construction, but it is perhaps to the graves of Wordsworth and his family that most visitors are drawn.

Alcock Tarn

Each year, on the Saturday nearest St Oswald's Day (5th August), Grasmere celebrates with a Rushbearing Ceremony, a custom that dates back to a time when the earthen floor of the church was strewn with fragrant rushes for warmth, cleanliness and to purify the air that was sometimes mildly foul from decaying corpses buried within the church. ●

Loughrigg Fell

		GPS waypoints
Start	Tarn Foot, Loughrigg	✏ NY 346 039
Distance	4½ miles (7.3km)	Ⓐ NY 343 049
Height gain	1,395 feet (425m)	Ⓑ NY 342 057
Approximate time	2½ hours	Ⓒ NY 356 058
Parking	Limited roadside parking	Ⓓ NY 356 043
Route terrain	Rough and confusing fell terrain; *do not attempt in poor visibility*	
Ordnance Survey maps	Landranger 90 (Penrith & Keswick), Explorer OL7 (The English Lakes – South-eastern area)	

Perched above Rydal Water and the lake at Grasmere, Loughrigg Fell throws down a challenge many cannot resist. Yet it is a complex and very confusing fell, a place of numerous hummocks and hollows, rocky outcrops, hidden dells and paths that twist in every direction. Only those competent in the use of map and compass should contemplate Loughrigg Fell in anything less than perfect conditions. *But it is on a fine, clear day that the rewards of this convoluted chaos will be best appreciated.*

Many ascents of Loughrigg Fell start from the north. Here, it is offered as an approach from the south, close by Loughrigg Tarn. This route has the advantage that the steep pull onto the fell places you within strides of the summit, and with the possibility of a speedy retreat if needed. On the complete circuit, a significant amount of up and down is involved throughout.

Rydal Water from Loughrigg Terrace

Start from the minor lane ascending from Skelwith Bridge, south of Loughrigg Tarn, and walk to the road junction; turn right to cross a bridge and then take the first turning on the left, a narrow lane leading to cottages. Bear right in front of the cottages, and on reaching Tarn Foot Lodge bear left through a gate onto a broad track that runs on to circle above the tarn. The view across the tarn of the Langdale Pikes is quite renowned.

Walk on past the cottages at The How, and about 100 yds farther on, leave the main track by branching right up to a gate. Through the gate, turn on to a path going off to the left (for Loughrigg Fell), and soon running alongside a moss-covered wall.

Just after a gate, and before a step-stile Ⓐ, abandon the main path and turn right to begin a steep ascent onto Loughrigg Fell. A stepped path climbs through a shallow ravine and, relaxing only as the top approaches, leads unerringly to a path junction at a large cairn, close to the summit of the fell, which lies just a short distance to the north-west. Turn left at the track and climb up to the trig pillar on the top of the fell, from which you can gain some idea of how complex the terrain is, but also enjoy outstanding views and some, like that of the Fairfield Horseshoe, viewed from an unfamiliar angle.

To continue, set off in a roughly north-westerly direction, following a clear path from just below the trig pillar. To get a general bearing, look for

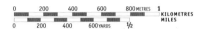

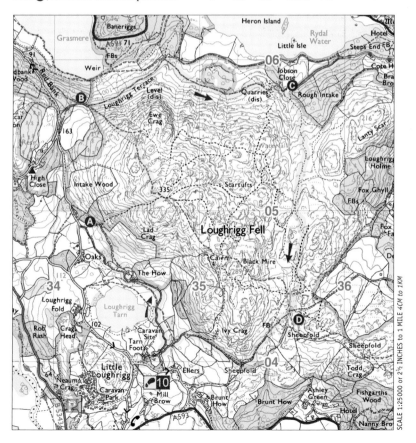

the lake of Grasmere and the road that climbs up to Dunmail Raise, and set off in that direction. The path descends steeply and comes down eventually to intercept a clear, horizontal path; this is Loughrigg Terrace **B**, which will convey you along the next section of the walk, offering lovely views across to Nab Scar and of Rydal Water.

The path runs on to cross a low ridge, and here you descend a little and then branch right, taking the higher of two paths. (There is an earlier shortcut to this section, and both tracks combine before reaching the edge of a small woodland.)

Keep following the terrace path, which runs on to reach the so-called Rydal Caves, although they actually mark the site of a disused slate mine. At the cavernous entrance, the main path zigzags down to the left. Follow this, shortly passing more caves, and a little farther on, cross a stream, and then turn immediately right, leaving the main track onto a rising path **C** that climbs onto the brackeny fellside above.

The next leg of the journey is the most confusing, so alertness on the part of at least one member of the party is vital to success.

When the path divides at NY 357 053, take the path second from the right – there are four paths diverging from this point. It helps if you have an idea of your general direction, and that is south. When the path forks again at NY 357 049, take the middle one of three possibilities, climbing a little farther until you can intercept a more prominent path, close by a large cairn.

Now turn right, heading in a south-westerly direction. When the track next divides, bear right towards a small tarn, close by which you intercept a broad track **D**. Turn right on this, as it now makes a steady descent around the southern edge of Loughrigg Fell.

As you round the end of the fell, so it brings the Langdale Pikes back into view, along with Bowfell, rising about Lingmoor Fell, and round to Swirl How, Wetherlam and the Old Man of Coniston.

The track gradually finds a way down to the valley farmland, and emerges at a gate adjoining Tarn Foot Lodge. Here cross a track and go forward past Dillygarth and the other cottages encountered on the outward route, to retrace your steps. ●

The summit of Loughrigg Fell

Elterwater

		GPS waypoints	
Start	Elterwater village		NY 328 048
Distance	5½ miles (8.9km)	Ⓐ	NY 341 034
Height gain	835 feet (255m)	Ⓑ	NY 330 029
Approximate time	2½ hours	Ⓒ	NY 313 035
Parking	Elterwater car park, just south of the Britannia Inn, or Elterwater Common, north of the village		
Route terrain	Riverside paths; farmland; woodland; some road walking		
Ordnance Survey maps	Landranger 90 (Penrith and Keswick), Explorer OL7 (The English Lakes – South-eastern area)		

Standing at the entrance to Langdale, and with the craggy Langdale Pikes as a backdrop, Elterwater is a cluster of attractive cottages, shops and an inn. The name of the village is said to mean 'Swan Lake' in Norse, and swans do indeed grace the nearby Elter Water from time to time. Surrounded by waterfalls, volcanic crags and tree-clad slopes, the village is largely built of the attractive, local grey-green stone, and centres on a small green with an ancient maple tree.

The village was once the focus of a thriving charcoal burning industry that used juniper wood, which was especially suitable for making gunpowder. The manufacture of gunpowder came to be an important Lakeland industry during the 18th century, and the gunpowder works at Elterwater did not close until the early 20th century.

🖉 Set off along the path to Skelwith (pronounced Skellith) Bridge from the river corner of the car park, a route that requires little description as it wanders on pleasantly to a superb resting place on the eastern shore of Elter Water. The Langdale Pikes rise across the tarn, their crags and gullies so intensely etched you can almost touch them.

Beyond the tarn, stay on the obvious path, passing through a gate close by the main road, and soon arriving at an attractive footbridge Ⓐ spanning the River Brathay. Cross the bridge to enter broad-leaved woodland, following a clear path that eventually leads round to join another, ascending from the left. Here, turn right, climbing gently through Bridge How Coppice.

At the top edge of the woodland, pass through another kissing-gate and continue on an obvious stony path that soon intercepts a rough vehicle access track. Turn right, following the track past a group of cottages and through two metal kissing-gates shortly to reach Elterwater Park Country Guest House.

Leave the buildings behind by following a waymarked path descending to a step-stile, and on to a gap-stile in a field corner. This gives

Elter Water and the Langdale Pikes

onto an enclosed path, at the end of which you cross to a metal kissing-gate. Follow an obvious path across a sloping field to a step-stile perched dramatically above the River Brathay.

The path that follows skims along the top of a steep drop to the river before descending by an awkward path to the riverside, and then crossing a small enclosure to a lane. Turn right for about 80 yds, and then leave the lane, on the left (signposted to High Park), by crossing two stiles adjoining the road **Ⓑ**. Bear immediately right on a permissive path to Colwith Force. As you approach, keep to the right of a fenced enclosure to reach a grandstand view of the falls.

Retrace your steps and walk around the enclosure, climbing to cross a low shoulder high above the falls. Now, follow a woodland path that sets off parallel with the river, but then moves away from it to rise to a gate in a wall. Through this, follow the continuing wall and soon turn right to walk across to High Park Farm. There turn left and go up to a lane, turning right and following the lane to Stang End, where

the road zigzags between buildings.

Stay on this quiet lane to the edge of woodland and then follow a broad track round to a footbridge spanning the Brathay. Do not cross the bridge, but instead go left beside the river on a rough track until, at a kissing-gate on the right, you can leave the track to approach nearby Slater Bridge.

Slater Bridge has to be the most eye-catching of the ancient bridges of Lakeland, humble and simple in its origins, but a masterpiece of poetry in construction. This two-part packhorse bridge, spanning the River Brathay, uses a large central rock and a long slab of rock to effect a link between Little Langdale and the slate quarries around Tilberthwaite.

Linger as you cross the bridge, but then keep straight ahead beside a wall

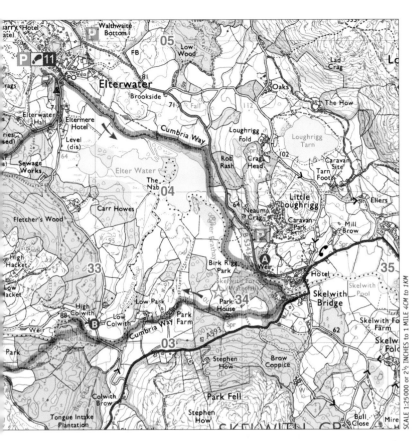

on your right (ignoring gaps and diverting pathways). The path rises with the wall, and provides an outstanding view to your left of Little Langdale Tarn and Greenburndale beyond. The path leads up to a farm access. Turn left and walk out to the Little Langdale road.

Go left again, but then immediately right onto a lane **C** that after another farm degenerates into a rough, stony track. Beyond a gate, as the track enters light woodland, keep right and continue descending, with increasing roughness underfoot, eventually to meet a lane leading

out to the Elterwater road. Turn left to return to the village. ●

Colwith Force

Rydal Water and Grasmere

		GPS waypoints
Start	Grasmere	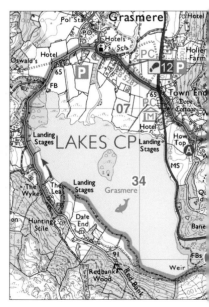 NY 339 073
Distance	5¼ miles (8.5km)	Ⓐ NY 344 068
Height gain	720 feet (220m)	Ⓑ NY 364 064
Approximate time	2½ hours	Ⓒ NY 348 060
Parking	Stock Lane car park (Pay and Display)	
Route terrain	Fell slope paths, rocky in places; lake shore paths; some road walking	
Ordnance Survey maps	Landranger 90 (Penrith and Keswick), Explorer OL7 (The English Lakes – South-eastern area)	

The presence of Wordsworth and his family imbue this walk with an air of poetic romance: two of his homes – Dove Cottage and Rydal Mount (details of which can be found on pages 94 & 95) – are passed en route. Rydal Water is where he used to skate, the surrounding fells are those from which he drew his inspiration, Grasmere is where he lies buried, and it is certain as can be that every step of the route will have been walked by Wordsworth, too.

The first stage of the walk uses an old corpse road linking Ambleside with Grasmere, while the return to Grasmere courts the shorelines of both Rydal Water and Grasmere lake.

Set off from the Stock Lane car park, turning left and walking out to the main valley road. Cross with care and walk into the narrow road opposite that soon passes Dove Cottage.

Wordsworth moved to Dove Cottage with his sister in 1799. The cottage was formerly an inn known as the 'Dove and Olive Bough', and first recorded in a list of pubs of Westmoreland in 1617, although there is another suggestion that it did not become an inn until the second half of the 18th century, and may well have been no more than an alehouse until then: it remained a pub until 1793. Another source suggests that what became Dove Cottage was

'Built in the early seventeenth century ... previously ... an inn, known as The Dove and Olive Bough, for travellers on the main road from Ambleside to Keswick.' In Grasmere in Wordsworth's Time, Eleanor Rawnsley describes 'The Dove and Olive Bough' as a 'house of call', namely a place, usually a public house, where journeymen connected with a particular trade assembled when out of work, ready for the call of employers; a kind of early-day job centre.

Rydal Water from the Corpse Road

Continue up the lane, ascending easily as far as a branching path on the left **Ⓐ**, next to a coffin stone at the western end of a corpse road that ran, in this instance, from Ambleside to St Oswald's Church in Grasmere.

Corpse roads were a route along which the dead were transported from remote communities to places with cemeteries and burial rights, such as parish churches. Not all communities had churches, and if the dead were to be buried in consecrated ground they had to be carried across country to the nearest church. Coffin stones, such as that here, where the route leaves the lane, were places on which the coffin might be rested for a while. There would have been a number of coffin stones along the route from Ambleside, but only this one remains – what appears to be a coffin stone adjacent to a seat later on in the walk, is in fact a memorial bench.

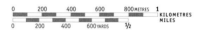

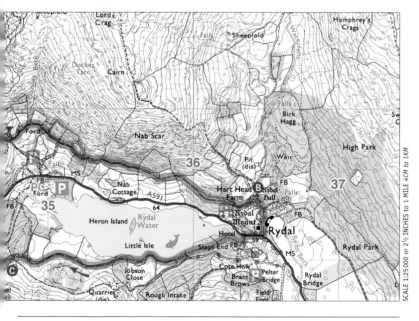

Leave the road here, by turning left and, keeping to the right of cottages, you soon join a path climbing gently through a scattering of trees to a bench at the junction of the route going off to Alcock Tarn. Join the surfaced lane behind the bench and walk up to pass a small pond (left) and a branching track down to White Moss (right). Keep ahead on the signposted Coffin Trail.

At Dunnabeck, the road surfacing ends and the track continues between walls, soon crossing Dunney Beck. As far as Brockstone Cottage the track is surfaced with slate gravel, but here the path narrows and becomes rougher underfoot as it crosses the top of another way down to White Moss. Go forward through a bridlegate, and now enjoy a delightful traverse of the steep lower slopes of Nab Scar. The route is easy to follow, crossing pasture and woodland, and undulating gently, with fine views across Rydal Water to Loughrigg Fell. Finally, a walled section leads out to a road head, with Rydal Mount immediately to the right **B**.

Originally built in the 16th century, possibly as a yeoman's cottage, Rydal Mount was home to the Wordsworth family from 1813 until the death of Mary Wordsworth in 1859, nine years after the poet's own death. It was the largest of the Wordsworthian homes and much-loved by the family. Over the years of his residence, as Juliet Barker points out in *Wordsworth: A Life,* Rydal Mount became 'a place of pilgrimage, not just for the great and powerful in church and state, but also more touchingly, for hundreds of ordinary people who came to pay their silent tribute to his genius.'

Turn down the lane, past Rydal Mount, to reach the main valley road. Just before reaching the road, you can turn into the churchyard and pass through to a gate giving into Dora's Field. This was where Wordsworth planned to build a house when threatened with eviction from Rydal Mount. But he was allowed to stay, and he later gave the field to his daughter, Dora. It is bright in springtime with daffodils planted as a memorial to Dora, who died in 1847.

Cross the road and turn right, and a short distance farther on, bear left down to a footbridge spanning the River Rothay.

Over the bridge take the path that bears off to the right, just above the river. The path soon brings Rydal Water into view, and after a metal kissing-gate enters light woodland. Continue following the path alongside Rydal Water and then eventually climb away from it above a wall, but always following a clear, ongoing path.

With Rydal Water now behind you, the path climbs briefly along the edge of a small copse to cross a narrow ridge **C** descending from Loughrigg Fell. Keep forward, crossing the ridge, and descending towards Grasmere lakeshore. The path brings you down to a footbridge spanning the outflow from the lake. Here, keep left, walking around the edge of the lake. Keep along the lakeshore, and then soon pass through a gate into light woodland.

Stay with the shoreline path for as long as possible, until turned inland at a boat house, to take a rough path climbing to meet the Red Bank road. Now, turn right and, taking care against approaching traffic, walk towards Grasmere.

As you come into the edge of Grasmere, take the Ambleside road to a T-junction near the church *(see Walk 9 for information about the church).* Turn right and past the church, then following the road (Stock Lane) back to the car park. ●

Tom Heights and Hodge Close

		GPS waypoints
Start	Glen Mary Bridge	✏ SD 322 999
Distance	5 miles (8km)	Ⓐ NY 328 005
Height gain	1,180 feet (360m)	Ⓑ NY 328 017
Approximate time	2½ hours	Ⓒ NY 323 028
Parking	Glen Mary Bridge car park	Ⓓ NY 319 019
Route terrain	Undulating walk through poorly drained terrain; slippery in places. Some minor road walking	Ⓔ NY 318 010
Ordnance Survey maps	Landrangers 90 (Penrith & Keswick) and 97 (Kendal to Morecambe), Explorer OL7 (The English Lakes – South-eastern area)	

This short walk is a little more demanding than might be supposed. It explores the area around the Hodge Close Quarries near Tilberthwaite, but involves a fair bit of undulating countryside. Even so, it is all very enjoyable, and takes you into a part of Lakeland that is comparatively neglected in favour of higher fells. It begins from the car park, traditionally known as Glen Mary Bridge, at the foot of Tom Gill, and climbs beside the gill to visit Tarn Hows.

✏ From the car park walk across to the nearby footbridge spanning Tom Gill, and, after a gate, ascend the true right bank of the stream through light woodland of birch. There are also small-leaved lime here, which is an ancient woodland indicator species, and the trees are thought to have been in this part of Lakeland since before Stonehenge was built.

On the way you pass first the lower of two Tom Gill waterfalls, attractive cascades in wooded ravines. The second appears a short distance farther on, and from the top of it, through a gate, you can walk up easily to reach the shores of Tarn Hows.

Turn left and follow a broad track beside the tarn. After about 250 yds a wire fence appears on the right, and just after it ends, leave the track by branching left onto a narrow path through bracken and birch, and climbing steeply. The path leads up to the knobbly top of Tom Heights Ⓐ, which is a surprisingly good vantage point with views southwards down the length of Coniston Water, north west into the Langdale valley and west to the main Coniston Fells.

The top of Tom Heights is a rash of boulders and heather, and has pretensions to mountain grandeur by boasting a couple of false summits before you get to the real thing.

Cross the summit and go down the other side, although the summit can be

Tarn Hows

by-passed on the right. Continue descending to reach a cross-path just before a small rise with a cairn. Here, turn right, descending north-east, steeply and boggily in places to reach a gate giving onto a walled stony track. Turn left along this for Oxen Fell and Langdales, and follow it out to meet a surfaced lane. Bear left, descending once more, to reach the main valley road at Mole End **B**.

Cross the road to enter the National Trust Oxen Fell plantation, and immediately turn right on a signposted footpath initially beside the road, crossing a footbridge and going through a kissing-gate to continue down a field edge. At another gate you rejoin the main road on the outskirts of Skelwith, but instantly turn left on a track bearing away from the road. This shortly joins a surfaced road at a junction. Take the right-hand road for High Park and Hallgarth.

The road undulates through pleasant scenery, and leads down to the cluster of buildings at High Park **C**. Stay on the road here, and press on for another 250 yds to a footpath sign on the left. Ascend left, on a broad grassy path to reach and pass a short stretch of moss-covered wall, beyond which you can cross to a step-stile at the end of a wall.

The next stretch is usually quite boggy, but there are enough rocks around to evade the worst clutches. Shortly after reaching the end of another wall, the path forks. Branch left, and a short way farther on, keep right when the path forks again to pass around the edge of a very boggy area. Keep following the ongoing path and eventually you meet a track just as it enters woodland at a gate.

Keep on into the woodland, following the track to Wythe Howe, the first of a small group of houses at Hodge Close. Pass through a gate and immediately bear left, uphill, passing a slate garage, and from it bearing left through another gate. You soon pass a weed-choked dam, and a short way on, at a signpost **D**, can turn right, through a gate to follow a track (fenced on the right) that leads around the rim of Hodge Close Quarry.

The path gradually descends towards another gate and stile, but ignore this, and, instead, bear left, climbing for a short while to another gate. Just a little way farther on, turn sharp left onto a path leading into a quarry area. A clear path leads through this, and climbs out on the other side, up to a reservoir.

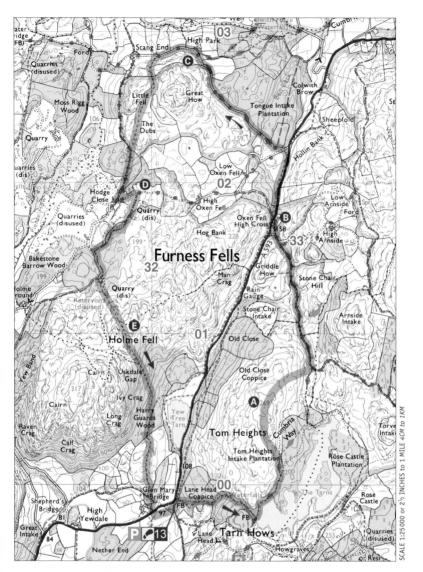

SCALE 1:25000 or 2½ INCHES to 1 MILE 4CM to 1KM

Cross the dam and follow the water's edge until, in effect, you are on the other side of the reservoir, and at the foot of a wide boggy gully.

Here, bear right, ascending the gully, doing your best to avoid the wet ground, and shortly climb to a col spanned by a collapsed wall **E**. Now go forward and begin descending. *This stretch is very rocky, and can be slippery when wet,* but it leads down to a path junction beside a cairn with a large boulder nearby. Turn right here,

and follow the path to Yew Tree Farm, which is preceded by a nice stand of Scots pine.

Go through a gate and down to the entrance to the **farm** (which has a **tearoom**). Walk out to the main road, and briefly cross to the right to a gate. Through this turn left along a field edge to another gate at the edge of the Glen Mary car park.

●

Pavey Ark and Harrison Stickle

Start	Great Langdale, New Dungeon Ghyll
Distance	3¾ miles (6km)
Height gain	2,200 feet (670m)
Approximate time	2½ hours
Parking	Stickle Ghyll car park (NT) (Pay and Display)
Route terrain	Rough fell walking; rocky ground; steep ascent and descent
Ordnance Survey maps	Landranger 90 (Penrith and Keswick), Explorer OL6 (The English Lakes – South-western area)

GPS waypoints

🖊 NY 294 064
Ⓐ NY 288 075
Ⓑ NY 285 079
Ⓒ NY 278 073

The Langdale Pikes in profile would have been as valid an icon for the National Park Authority as that of Wasdale Head, possibly more so. They appear somewhere from almost every walk in this book, shapely, striking, seductive and hugely distinctive. Harrison Stickle is the highest of the Pikes, and its ascent gives access to other fells nearby – Loft Crag, Pike of Stickle, Thunacar Knott, Sergeant Man, High Raise, and, as embraced in this walk, Pavey Ark.

🖊 Start from the Stickle Ghyll car park in Great Langdale by walking up to the left of the buildings at the rear of the car park to follow a brief, enclosed path that leads out to a junction of paths at Stickle Ghyll. Where the track divides, bear right beside the ghyll to locate a path leading to a bridge spanning the watercourse. There has been considerable and much-needed path improvement work on the route up to Stickle Tarn, which not so long ago was in places a rock-clutching stagger. It is still a rough path, but it leads unerringly up to the tarn Ⓐ set against the breathtaking backdrop of Pavey Ark. Not until the very last moment does the uphill collarwork cease, but when it does, the sense of relief is considerable.

The dark cliffs of Pavey Ark are inspiring and intimidating, and no place for walkers. Close observation will enable you to pick out an ascending line from the bottom right of the cliffs to near the top left. This is Jack's Rake, a breeze for some, but nonetheless a moderate rock climb and so beyond the scope of this book, although most walkers are tempted to venture into its embrace sooner or later.

For the present keep to the right of Stickle Tarn, and then ascend a little along Bright Beck before crossing it in search of the North Rake, although it actually runs north-eastwards. Initially it is out of sight, but simply stick with Bright Beck until you see much easier

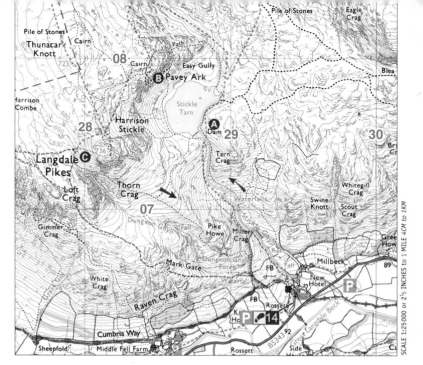

ground to your left, and then cross the beck and begin a steady plod onto Pavey Ark **B**. A clear day will improve your chances of hitting the rocky summit of Pavey Ark rather than the rather unappealing mound that is Thunacar Knott.

The onward route lies to the south-west, a clear path heading for Harrison Stickle, and it is well to get the direction firmly in mind, as many paths have materialised over the years across the intervening ground, notably one ascending from the southern edge of Stickle Tarn.

As you cross to Harrison Stickle, a path does lead the way, but, on a clear day, there is much fun in diverting onto rocky ribs and knobbly outcrops, although there is no path this way. The final pull to the top of Harrison Stickle is straightforward, and brings with it respite from all uphill work and a commanding view of considerable merit.

The way down lies to the south, but that is certainly not the way to set off, as it leads only into untold difficulties and danger. The safest, indeed the only,

way is to set off initially in a northerly direction, as if heading for Thunacar Knott, but then curving to the west and south-west into the boggy hollow of Harrison Combe at the top of Dungeon Ghyll **C**. There is a prominent scree path that leaves Harrison Stickle summit in a westwards direction, and leads to the same patch of marshy ground, but it is easier just to give this a wide berth.

From Harrison Combe, a clear but narrow path now leads across the upper clutches of Dungeon Ghyll, and requires careful progress.

Once beyond the initial section, the going becomes much easier as you descend steadily towards, and then to the right of Pike Howe. The path has had repair work undertaken in recent years, and leads down to a wall and a stile. Keep following the ensuing wall to reach a gate beyond which a stony path leads back towards Stickle Ghyll and the small area of woodland at New Dungeon Ghyll. ●

Pike o'Blisco and Cold Pike

Start	Three Shire Stone, Wrynose	
Distance	3¾ miles (6km)	
Height gain	1,675 feet (510m)	
Approximate time	2½ hours	
Parking	near Three Shire Stone	
Route terrain	Rough fell country	
Ordnance Survey maps	Landranger 90 (Penrith and Keswick), Explorer OL6 (The English Lakes – South-western area)	

GPS waypoints

🥾 NY 277 027
Ⓐ NY 267 039
Ⓑ NY 263 036

The two seemingly innocuous fells either side of Red Tarn are arguably the source of the River Duddon, although Red Tarn itself contrives to send its waters in the other direction, northwards into Mickleden. As a rule, both summits are ignored by walkers bound for Crinkle Crags, but they are worthy of anyone's attention, and will place demands on navigational ability if the weather closes in.

🥾 From the parking area near the Three Shire Stone join an obvious path that heads north up the lower slopes of Pike o'Blisco. Keep along the main path and cross a tributary of the embryonic River Duddon. Eventually the gradient eases and there are numerous places where you can relax and take a breather.

More ascent follows, but is short-lived. Pike o'Blisco presses in on your right and Cold Pike on your left. Gradually, Crinkle Crags comes into view, its undulating profile looking rather like a rippling serpent on the skyline.

After climbing for a while, the path levels again and you see the full length of the reed-fringed Red Tarn. The path keeps well above the tarn, and leads beyond it to an area of red shale Ⓐ, close by the point where the outlet from the tarn heads for Browney Gill and down into Oxendale.

From this minor col, a part-pitched, part-gravel path leads up onto Pike o'Blisco, which has two 'summits', each with a large cairn, the more northerly being the higher. There is a splendid view from here of Crinkle

Pike o'Blisco

Crags in particular.

Return down the path towards Red Tarn, and cross the Red Tarn outflow, and then continue up another part-pitched path, with Great Knott towering to your right. With time in hand, it is always worth making a detour to Great Knott for the outstanding views it affords, and being off the main track, it is a good place to take a breather.

Back on the main path, and just before a cairn that marks the point where the path winds right to head for Crinkle Crags, you need to take an indistinct path going left, just before a stream. Although easy to miss, a grassy path soon becomes clear as it climbs steadily. Pass two cairns along the ridge and then follow a steeper path through rock outcrops and huge blocks of rock to finally reach the summit of Cold Pike **B**.

The onward route, down to the Three Shire Stone is confusing in poor visibility, when a retreat by the outward route is probably preferable. With good visibility and confidence, however, you can head in a south-easterly direction,

descending all the while. The precise line is anything but precise, and you should make your own route, dodging around rock outcrops as necessary and, if anything, trending more to the left (east) than the right, which if you go too far will drop you into the craggy mess that is Wrynose Breast.

Eventually, the descent eases and you encounter a path that crosses the valley floor, taking you across marshy ground towards your line of ascent. At a small stream, step across on boulders and carry on the grassy path as it heads down towards the Pass. Carry on to the next feeder stream, a wider one, which is easily crossed, and climb the slope beyond.

As you near the main path the ground becomes quite wet and the path all but vanishes. Here you will need to pick your way across. Keep on to join the main path and turn right at a small cairn to retrace your outwards steps back to the parking area. ●

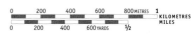

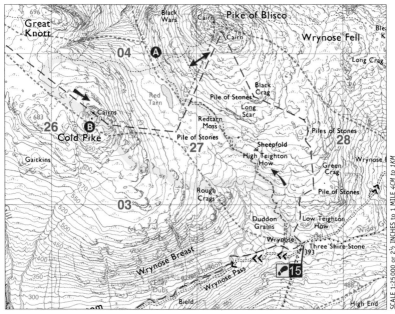

Wray Castle and Blelham Tarn

		GPS waypoints
Start	Red Nab, High Wray	
Distance	6 miles (9.7km)	SD 385 995
Height gain	785 feet (240m)	Ⓐ NY 376 013
Approximate time	3 hours	Ⓑ NY 371 009
Parking	At start	Ⓒ NY 362 004
Route terrain	Lakeshore paths; farmland; woodland; some road walking	Ⓓ SD 372 999
		Ⓔ SD 375 989
		Ⓕ SD 378 986
Ordnance Survey maps	Landrangers 90 (Penrith & Keswick) and 97 (Kendal & Morecambe), Explorer OL7 (The English Lakes – South-eastern area)	

A chance to walk on the quiet side of Windermere, exploring a landscape that would have been familiar to Beatrix Potter, and which almost certainly sowed seeds in her imagination that later grew into her successful series of books. There is a great peace about this walk, which visits both Wray Castle, where Potter stayed as a child, and the beautifully set Blelham Tarn.

Begin from the parking area at Red Nab, at the shoreline end of the road from High Wray, and set off northwards along a broad lakeshore path and at the edge of broad-leaved Arthur Wood. In the woodland, sessile oak is the dominant tree species with an understorey of birch, holly and hazel, but there is also ash, wych elm and bird cherry. Great spotted woodpeckers favour these woodlands and it is a rare day when you do not see or at least hear them. There is also a good deal of evidence that the woodland was coppiced to produce charcoal for iron smelting and the manufacture of gunpowder. Tree bark was also used in the leather tanning process.

On leaving the woodland you arrive at High Wray Bay. Continue to a gate and through this carry on for another 45 yds to a second gate giving onto a permitted path into the grounds of Wray Castle. Return to the shore of the lake, and shortly climb left up a slope. At the top, bear right to a stile/gate to re-enter woodland, beyond which lies shapely Watbarrow Point sticking out into the lake like a knobbly thumb.

When the path intercepts another at a T-junction at Low Wray Bay Ⓐ, turn left onto a gravel path that leads up towards Wray Castle.

Before doing so, a short diversion to the right is in order to visit the handsome Wray Castle Boathouse, which houses some of the fine ancient steamers that ply the lake. You can also make a short circuit of nearby Calf Parrock Coppice if time permits. You enter at a gate and can make an easy circular walk clockwise or anticlockwise.

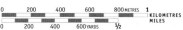

SCALE 1:25000 or 2½ INCHES to 1 MILE 4CM to 1KM

| 0 | 200 | 400 | 600 | 800 METRES | 1 |
| 0 | 200 | 400 | 600 YARDS | ½ | |

KILOMETRES
MILES

Continue up the track, alongside a fence to just below the edifice of Wray Castle, and here turn right, still following a fenceline and on a path for the Gatehouse and Blelham Tarn. The path leads you up steps to the main entrance to the castle.

Wray Castle, then in the ancient county of Lancashire, was the creation of Dr James Dawson, a Liverpool surgeon who built the castle in 1840-7. There are towers, turrets, machicolations and battlements everywhere and a vast coach door (porte cochère), a feature of many 19th-century mansions. For that is what Wray Castle is, a mansion, built with the fortune of Dawson's wife, who alas did not like the building and refused to live in it. Beatrix Potter stayed at the castle when she was 16, and later bought much of the surrounding land, although she never owned the castle.

The castle, owned by the National Trust, is only very occasionally open to the public, although the grounds are freely accessible. They contain some outstanding tree specimens including Wellingtonia, redwood, weeping lime and Ginkgo biloba (also known as the Maidenhair Tree), a unique tree with no close-living relatives.

Continue out from the castle, along its surfaced driveway to reach the

High Wray Bay, Windermere

gatehouse, although it is possible to briefly divert into the ground of Wray church (also built by Dawson), where Hardwicke Rawnsley, co-founder of the National Trust, was vicar from 1877 until 1883.

At the road, turn right, descending gently. As the road starts to climb again, just after passing the turning to Low Wray campsite, go through a kissing-gate on the left **B** and along a permitted path beside the road. After 200 yds you arrive at a road gate on your right. Here, turn left onto a bridleway that passes to the south of a hummock known as Randy Pike. When the track forks, bear left across a hummocky pasture on a broad grassy path that leads to a gate giving into sparse broad-leaved woodland. The track leads to a shallow ford, crossed on stepping stones, just after which you keep to the left of a wall to enter the next pasture. The path stays by the wall to reach another permitted footpath at a signpost **C**.

Turn left for High Tock How, following a path around the south-western end of Blelham Tarn that soon runs alongside a fence. The path crosses a neat stone bridge after which it rises as a broad track to a stone barn. Just past the barn, cross a step-stile onto a path for High Tock How. Walk up to another gate and beyond this descend around the edge of rough pasture to the access to the farm. Turn right to walk out to a lane. Turn right again, climbing briefly to a higher road.

Turn left, and now follow the road, taking care against approaching traffic, for $\frac{1}{2}$ mile, passing an interesting stone-built well 'In Memory of Happy Days', built in 1891.

The roadside hedge has been used for the traditional boundary building technique of hedge laying, a country skill found throughout Britain and Ireland.

As you reach High Wray Farm, leave the road by branching right onto a roughly surfaced track **D** signposted for Basecamp and Claife Heights. Continue past the turning into Basecamp, now following a broad woodland trail. Ignore diverging footpaths and stay on the main trail, climbing steadily for some distance into an area that has been cleared. Gradually the trail starts to descend, and when the track forks **E** bear left, taking the lower of two trails.

At a multiple track junction **F**, turn left onto a bridleway for Belle Grange. The track, which is quite rough underfoot, descends through splendid, mature mixed woodland. At the next path junction, continue descending towards the lakeshore.

The track eventually comes down to reach the boundary wall of Belle Grange, which is followed out to intercept the lakeshore path. Turn left for High Wray, and follow the track back to the Red Nab car park. ●

Grisedale Tarn

Start	Mill Bridge, Grasmere	**GPS waypoints**	
Distance	5 miles (8km)	NY 336 090	
Height gain	1,900 feet (580m)	**A** NY 339 098	
Approximate time	3 hours	**B** NY 348 112	
Parking	Limited roadside parking near start		
Route terrain	Rough fell paths		
Ordnance Survey maps	Landranger 90 (Penrith & Keswick), Explorer OL5 (The English Lakes – North-eastern area)		

The whole of this walk forms part of the Northern Coast-to-Coast long-distance trail, originally pioneered by Wainwright, but since honed by other writers, the author included, into arguably the most popular trail in Britain. This brief introduction, and out-and-back route visits lonely, fell-girt Grisedale Tarn, a splendid location, surrounded by high fells, and one that holds out the prospect of discovering royal treasure.

There is limited roadside parking alongside the A591 just south of Mill Bridge, on the northbound side of the road. From here, walk northwards for a short distance, and cross the road with care to enter a bridleway (for Patterdale) running alongside cottages and soon becoming enclosed between walls as it climbs to a gate.

Beyond the gate, the track continues to climb for a while, but then levels as it approaches a group of sheep pens at the tip of an interesting geological divide known as the Great Tongue. Close by there is a confluence of down-rushing streams **A**; that on the right is to host the line of ascent.

Begin by crossing the first stream, Little Tongue Gill, and then the next, Tongue Gill. Beyond, you plug into a fine rising path, going up in easy stages, and with fine retrospective views of the Langdale Pikes, Crinkle Crags and the Coniston Fells. Gradually, the path closes in on waterfalls near the top of the gill, and reaches a brief rock step, crossed by a series of ledges and a rough, stony path.

Cross the stream ahead, and tackle a constructed pathway **B** across rough

Grisedale Tarn

ground to a false col, beyond which you will see a shallow basin that almost certainly once held a tarn. Continue around its left edge and climb to the true col, Grisedale Hause. Grisedale Hause is a marvellous setting. Ahead and below Grisedale Tarn reposes in a great bowl. To your left Seat Sandal rises craggily, to your right Fairfield does so, too, as if daring you to divert onto its scree and rock slopes. Beyond the tarn the prominent summit is Dollywaggon Pike, the precursor of the long ridge rising up to Helvellyn.

You can turn round from Grisedale Hause, to set off back if you wish. But there is merit in taking the slanting path that leads down to the outflow of the tarn, especially on a fine day when its various nooks and crannies offer shelter and the chance to nod off for a while sequestered in a most magical setting.

Grisedale Tarn was the subject of a poem by the Reverend Father Frederick Faber, who described the hollow,

'Where waveless Grisedale lies,
And the three clefts of grassy fell
Let in the blueness of the skies;
And lowland sounds come travelling up.'

But the tarn's appeal lies in legend, distorted and confused though it is. Here, the crown of Duvenald, the last king of Cumberland, is said to have been cast following his defeat by the combined forces of Edmund of Northumbria and Malcolm of Scotland. The crown has never been recovered, but as the tarn is over 98 feet deep that is not surprising. In reality, as a royal crown would be regarded as the plunder of war, it is unlikely that anyone would be throwing it away.

The large pile of stones on the A591 at the top of Dunmail Raise is said to be where the king lies buried. Whether that is so is unknown; the battle in which the king is supposed to have been killed took place in the year 945, yet learned authorities have it that Dunmail

Ascending to Grisedale Tarn

died on pilgrimage to Rome in 975. There is a path, albeit a wet one, all around the tarn, should you wish to make the circuit. Either way, to effect the return to Grasmere you need to retreat to Grisedale Hause. Strong walkers might want to divert briefly onto the summit of Seat Sandal, which can be accomplished with care from the hause.

Otherwise, set off back down the path used on the ascent, but at the point above the waterfalls where the path forks, keep to the right, and now head down Little Tongue Gill, using the route that Victorians would take to make the ascent of Helvellyn.

This steady descent leads easily down to the gate near the sheep pens, from which you simply retrace your outward route to the A591. ●

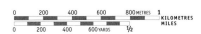

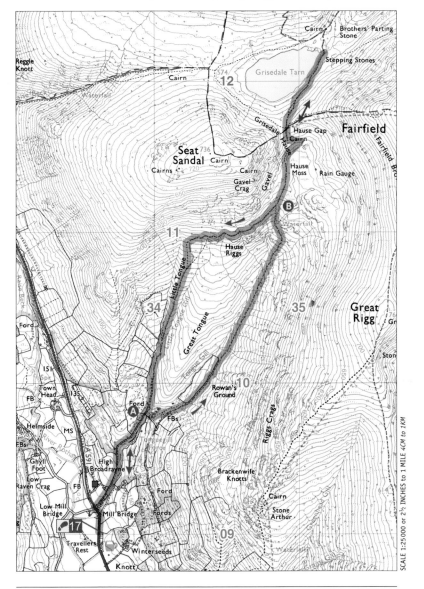

Tarn Hows

		GPS waypoints
Start	Hawkshead	

Start	Hawkshead	
Distance	6 miles (9.5km)	
Height gain	985 feet (300m)	
Approximate time	3 hours	
Parking	Hawkshead (Pay and Display)	
Route terrain	Farmland; woodland; fell tracks; some road walking	
Ordnance Survey maps	Landrangers 90 (Penrith & Keswick) and 97 (Kendal & Morecambe), Explorer OL7 (The English Lakes – South-eastern area)	

GPS waypoints

- ✐ SD 354 980
- Ⓐ SD 335 990
- Ⓑ SD 327 998
- Ⓒ NY 331 007
- Ⓓ SD 342 994
- Ⓔ SD 350 986

Hawkshead is laden with Wordsworth and Beatrix Potter memorabilia, and as a result has become a tourist-saturated hot spot at certain times of year. Yet without these literary associations, Hawkshead would still attract visitors for its splendid architecture, its lovely setting, ancient pubs and an air of tranquility. Not far away lies Tarn Hows, another popular tourist destination, so linking the two, as this walk does, is both logical and attractive. Out of season the area is quieter, but you are never likely to tackle this walk without company somewhere in sight.

Chapel, Hawkshead Hill

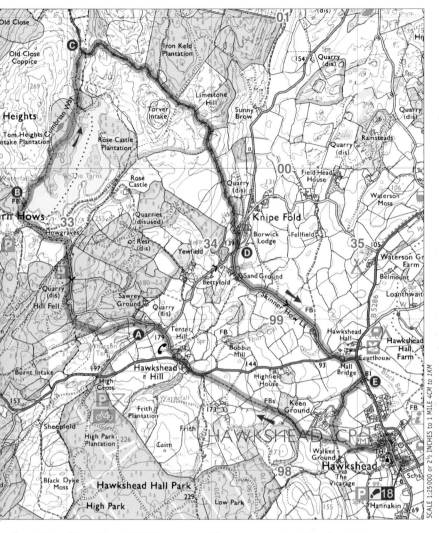

SCALE 1:25000 or 2½ INCHES to 1 MILE 4CM to 1KM

```
0    200   400   600   800 METRES   1
                                     KILOMETRES
                                     MILES
0    200   400   600 YARDS   ½
```

Walk into the centre of Hawkshead, immediately passing the Grammar School attended by Wordsworth. Stroll along Main Street and pass the **Queen's Head** to reach the Beatrix Potter Gallery *(details of which can be found on page 94),* now housed in the former offices of her husband, William Heelis, a local solicitor.

Turn left in front of the gallery, passing to the rear of the **Kings Arms hotel**, and going into Vicarage Lane.

You soon pass Ann Tyson's cottage, where Wordsworth boarded. Now follow the ongoing lane out of Hawkshead and continue to a footpath on the right, signposted for Tarn Hows. Turn through a gate and follow a path across a pasture, and up to a gate. Go forward towards and along the edge of mixed woodland.

Shortly the path runs alongside a stream, which it crosses by a footbridge, after which it scampers rockily up to a gate at the top edge of the woodland. A clear path now leads on across a large pasture, and eventually comes down to meet a road near Hawkshead Hill.

Turn left along the road, walk into the village and then take the first lane on the right (just after the chapel). At the next road junction, keep left. After passing Summer Hill turn right along a narrow lane for Tarn Hows, and shortly leave the lane through a kissing-gate on the left **Ⓐ**. Follow a continuing path above the road, which crosses two rough pastures, climbing steadily. On the far side of the second field, go through the right-hand one of two kissing-gates to enter an area of light broad-leaved woodland.

The path climbs steadily through the woodland, never far from the road to Tarn Hows which, at one point it almost rejoins, but instead descends into a stand of mature larch. The path does finally come back out onto the road, where Tarn Hows now eases into view. Bear left down the road for a short distance until you can take a clear grassy path going off on the right towards the tarn.

The path comes down to intercept a broad surfaced track that circles around the tarn. Turn left on this and follow this or a slightly lower path to the southern edge of the tarn. Pass through a gate and across the top of the path ascending via Tom Gill **Ⓑ**. Keep on along the western tarnside path, at varying distances from it until, as you approach the northern end of the tarn, leave the main path, and branch left at a signpost for Arnside and the Langdales. This path cuts through light woodland, mainly birch, below Tom Heights.

The path ends at a kissing-gate where it gives on to a broad stony track **Ⓒ**. Turn right for Iron Keld and Hawkshead.

The trail is a Byway Open to All Traffic, so take care against vehicles, usually motor bikes that use it from time to time. The track climbs at first, but soon levels and sets off in splendid fashion across hummocky terrain. Once beyond the turning into the Iron Keld Plantation the track starts to descend and provides lovely forward views embracing quite a panorama from Esthwaite Water, across Claife Heights and Latterbarrow, to the distant Howgills, the low fells beyond Windermere, Wansfell set against the Kentmere Fells, Stony Cove Pike and Red Screes above Kirkstone and Little Hart Crag, at the head of Scandale, tucked in between Red Screes and the eastern arm of the Fairfield Horseshoe.

The track eventually comes down to join the road near Borwick Lodge. Cross the road and go immediately left along the side lane for Hawkshead **Ⓓ**, taking care against approaching traffic on this narrow lane. The lane descends to intercept a road. Turn left and take particular note of the architecture of the cottages nearby, which have large circular chimneys, and the curious stone-built structure off to the left, which is the Hawkshead Courthouse.

Hawkshead Courthouse is all that remains of a medieval farm that belonged to Furness Abbey until the Dissolution of the Monasteries in 1537. Hawkshead Hall Farm, formerly Hawkshead Old Hall, was part of the monastic grange.

The road comes down to meet the B5286. Turn right, and then at Keen Ground Lodge leave the road for a driveway on the right **Ⓔ** for Walker Ground. As you reach the entrance to Keen Ground, go left through a gate and immediately right to a waymark. From this bear diagonally left across a hummocky pasture to a gate and kissing-gate from which an indistinct grassy path cuts across the slope of another field, to a step-stile at which you intercept the outward route. Here turn left beside a fence and retrace your steps to Hawkshead village. ●

Claife Heights

Start	Windermere (west shore)	**GPS waypoints**
Distance	6¾ miles (11km)	🥾 SD 388 954
Height gain	1,265 feet (385m)	Ⓐ SD 378 956
		Ⓑ SD 375 959
Approximate time	3½ hours	Ⓒ SD 377 982
Parking	Old quarry car park (National Trust Pay and Display)	Ⓓ SD 383 974
		Ⓔ SD 382 959
Route terrain	Farmland; woodland; a little road walking	
Ordnance Survey maps	Landranger 97 (Kendal & Morecambe) Explorer OL7 (The English Lakes – South-eastern area)	

This walk sets out to explore the afforested slopes of Claife Heights, but tends to get amiably distracted as it wanders across to Far Sawrey first, and then by way of some delectable tarns and almost park-like farmland before finally yielding to the pull of the trees.

🥾 Start from the car park just beside the ferry road on the way to Far Sawrey and take to a path above the road (signposted for Near Sawrey). The

Moss Eccles Tarn

path soon comes out onto the road. Cross, and continue on the other side along a path starting at the top end of Ash Landing Nature Reserve. This path, too, soon comes out on the road, at the edge of Far Sawrey. Walk up the road, but after about 100 yds leave it at a bend by turning right through gate pillars and onto a stony track for Hill Top. This leads up to cross the end of a surfaced lane, near a farm.

Continue through the kissing-gate opposite and walk up beside a wall towards a cottage, after which you take a waymarked route past more cottages and Sawrey Knotts. There is a fine view ahead of the Old Man of Coniston. From Brimstock Cottage, the route descends on a broad track to reach the road again not far from **Sawrey Hotel**. Walk past the hotel, and on the far side of the village leave the road by branching right past The Glen onto a bridleway Ⓐ for Moss Eccles Tarn.

At a signpost Ⓑ, leave the surfaced

Wise Een Tarn and the Langdale Pikes

lane by branching left onto a stony track that leads to a footbridge and ford, continuing on the other side through farmland that has an almost parkland feel to it. Keep following the track roughly in a northerly direction and eventually you emerge just above Moss Eccles Tarn.

Beatrix Potter bought Moss Eccles Tarn in 1913, the year that she became Mrs William Heelis. The tarn forms part of the Claife Tarns and Mires Site of Special Scientific Interest by virtue of its wide range of aquatic and wetland plants, and for damselflies and dragon flies. The water lilies that brighten its surface in the summer are said to have been the inspiration for the great children's favourite, *The Tale of Mr Jeremy Fisher.*

Continue with the track past the tarn, and keep following the main route, which starts to climb above Moss Eccles Tarn. At a gate, Wise Een Tarn suddenly comes into view, set against a backdrop of Langdale. The track passes a smaller tarn (Scale Head Tarn), with a dam wall, after which it starts climbing towards the trees of Claife Heights.

Keep following the track as it climbs towards the woodland and then runs alongside a wall. At a gate you finally enter the plantation, continuing on a clear path and shortly passing a shallow tarn on the right (High Moss Tarn).

About 300 yds farther on at a bridleway waymark, stay on the main track descending on the right to a path junction at a signpost **C**. Here leave the main track and branch right onto a footpath for the Ferry and Far Sawrey. The path now plunges deeply into forest, where, not surprisingly, roots hamper progress, and where the odds on losing your sense of direction at least once are better than average. But the path does lead out to another signpost, which indicates the ongoing path that now runs up the edge of a fairly young plantation.

Although the path is rough and ready it is nevertheless constant, and leads you up to the top edge of the forest from which there are fine views extending from the Coniston Fells, all the way round past the Kentmere Fells to the distant Howgills. The path climbs to a rocky topknot with a superb view. From here plunge downwards back into forest. Eventually the path comes down to merge with a broad forest trail at a signpost and close by shallow

Brownstone Tarn.

Turn right and walk along the trail, but after about 100 yds leave it for a path on the left returning to mature plantation. The woodlands hereabouts and down to a point above the ferry station are host to an ancient tale. On a stormy night, some time in the 15th century, the ferryman heard a call from above the shore and rowed across to investigate. He returned alone, terrified

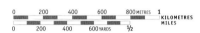

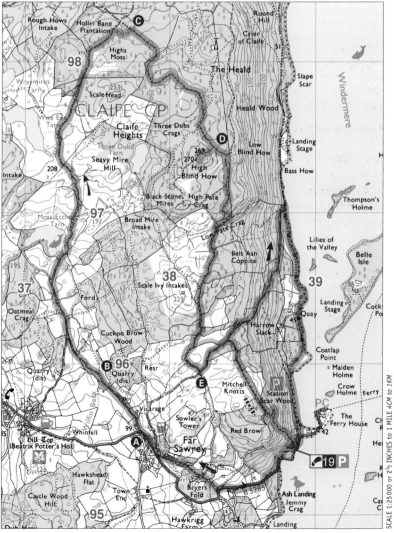

and unable to speak, becoming so ill with a fever that he died a few days later. For years afterwards, no ferryman would tend the ferry after dark. The voice, which became known as the Crier of Claife, was exorcised by a monk from Furness Abbey, but it is said that there are still locals who will not venture into the woods at night.

When the path forks **D**, you can divert briefly to the right and climb to the trig pillar on High Blind How, the highest point of Claife Heights. It is, perhaps, one of the finest stone-built trig pillars, and sits on a neat rocky plinth surround by trees in all directions. Go back to the path junction and there turn right to continue the descent.

Eventually the path comes to run alongside a wall; if you go through a gap in the wall you get a lovely view over the lake of Windermere to Bowness. It is tempting to speculate that this may well have been the spot to which the young Wordsworth would come with friends from the school in Hawkshead. Of course, the trees that cloak the fells today would not have been there in Wordsworth's day, and he may not have needed to go any farther than High Blind How to be able to watch the ancient ferry crossing the lake.

Stay within the forest boundary and not far from the wall, to locate a three-way signpost. Continue with the path for Far Sawrey, which drops abruptly as it crosses High and Low Pate Crags, both of which are somewhat ambitious names for what are really glacially shaped rock bands. But they are distinctive, and the path does a slight fandango to get around them.

A short way farther on, the path takes an enclosed route between a moss-covered wall and a fence as you now start to move out of the main body of the forest into an area more lightly wooded. The view remains extensive and now extends as far as Ingleborough and Whernside in the Yorkshire Dales.

At a gate you finally break free from woodland to go forward on a farm track beside a wall. This finally descends between walls to a junction **E**. Here, turn left. When you reach a footpath through a kissing-gate on the right, you can go this way to make a more direct return to the start. But otherwise, to enjoy a stroll along the shore of Windermere, simply keep ahead, soon passing through a gate and entering an area of light woodland, through which the path descends steadily.

The path is leading you in the wrong direction but brings you down towards the lakeshore. Just before the path bottoms out, you can go right over a step-stile to effect a little shortcut down to the surfaced lane that runs along the shoreline. Turn right on this and follow it out to the ferry road.

Just as you reach the road, go a few strides farther forward and then turn right, up steps onto a signposted path for Hill Top via Sawrey. Climb with the path to a signpost where you can turn left and go down steps that once served Claife Station. At the bottom of the steps, turn right to return to the car park.

Just above the ferry station on the west shore of Windermere are the ruins of Claife Station, one of Thomas West's 'stations' from which visiting Victorians might best perceive the view across the lake. It was built in the 1790s, but was most fashionable in the first half of the 19th century. The building had windows of tinted glass of different colours to vary the experience according to the weather, and to create different lighting effects: yellow for summer, orange for autumn, light green for spring and light blue for winter. There was also dark blue for moonlight and lilac, which was intended to give the impression of a thunderstorm. ●

Wansfell Pike

		GPS waypoints
Start	Salutation Inn, Ambleside	✏ NY 377 045
Distance	6 miles (9.5km)	Ⓐ NY 403 040
Height gain	1,837 feet (560m)	Ⓑ NY 407 026
Approximate time	3½ hours	Ⓒ NY 397 024
Parking	Various Pay and Display car parks around the centre of Ambleside	Ⓓ NY 384 028
Route terrain	Rough fell, but with good tracks and paths throughout most of the route	
Ordnance Survey maps	Landranger 90 (Penrith & Keswick), Explorer OL7 (The English Lakes –South-eastern area)	

Wansfell Pike is not the highest point of the wedge of ground between Ambleside and the village of Troutbeck, but it has long been popular as a viewpoint, especially down the length of Windermere and north-eastwards to the fells above Kentmere. This circuit begins in the centre of Ambleside, at the Salutation Inn, and then crosses Wansfell Pike to slip down into the Troutbeck Valley. Wansfell has strong connections to Ambleside and is seen as very much belonging to the town. Local author and climber, Bill Birkett considers that 'Wansfell is to Ambleside what St Paul's is to London'.

✏ Leave Ambleside just by the **Salutation Inn** by following a narrow lane (signposted for Stock Ghyll: Wansfell Pike and the Waterfalls), and very soon reach Stock Ghyll. The Salutation is one of the oldest inns in Ambleside.

The road climbs gently and continues to the entrance to Stock Ghyll Park *(see Walk 1)*. Turn left here to follow Stock Ghyll upstream; red waymarkers point the way to a viewing platform for the falls. If you prefer to leave a visit to the falls for another day, ignore this turning and simply stay on the road, rejoining the route at a cattle-grid.

Stock Ghyll was hugely popular in Victorian times, with visitors coming in good numbers to view the falls. Near

the top of the falls, as you reach a junction of paths, turn right. A sign points the way to a revolving gate. Go through the gate and turn left along the lane. About 150 yds after a cattle-grid at the entrance to Grove Farm, cross a step-stile in the wall on your right (signed for Troutbeck via Wansfell). Follow the surfaced path uphill along the left-hand of a hill pasture parallel with a stream, to a kissing-gate giving on to Access Land.

From here, the ascent is steeper and now follows a stepped pathway built in the 1990s to combat erosion. As you close in on the summit of Wansfell, a footbridge crosses the stream, with the route still continuing as a stepped path, gradually moving away from the stream.

On the summit of Wansfell Pike, cross a ladder-stile and then descend with a clear path, which slips down easily to pass through a wall at a kissing-gate. Walkers wanting to visit Baystones to the north-east, should simply follow the wall in that direction, and then descend around walls but generally in a southerly direction to intercept a walled track (Nanny Lane). The grassy lump of Baystones, although higher than Wansfell Pike, does not have anything like the same views, but, for those keen on ticking lists, it now ranks as a Marilyn, one of the 'Relative Hills of Britain', with a height of 1,601 feet (488m).

A short way farther on along the original line of descent, the route meets a walled lane at a gate **A**. This is a lower section of Nanny Lane. Turn right into the lane and follow it down into the Troutbeck Valley.

On reaching Troutbeck village, turn right and follow the village road, the

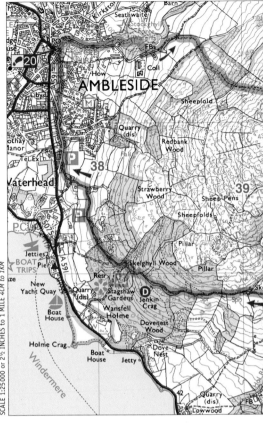

The Coniston Fells from the top of Wansfell

original route through Troutbeck as evidenced by a number of drinking troughs at the side of the road placed for the refreshment of horses pulling coaches up the road en route from Windermere to Penrith.

The village of Troutbeck consists largely of 17th-, 18th- and 19th-century houses ranged along a narrow road just above the valley bottom. One of the first buildings you encounter is Hoggart's House, named after playwright Thomas Hogarth, who used to live here. Some of the buildings have retained the original features such as mullioned windows and a rare example of an exposed spinning gallery. Beatrix Potter used to live in the village at Troutbeck Park Farm,

highest point, having been continually ascending since Troutbeck.

The path leads down to meet the Low Skelghyll track at a couple of gates beside Hol Beck. Here, turn right through a kissing-gate onto a surfaced lane leading up to High Skelghyll. Continue past High Skelghyll Farm and on the other side take the lower of two ongoing tracks. Continue into the woodland of Jenkins Crag, and shortly taking a brief diversion to the viewpoint of the crag itself **D**. Then continue along the forest trail.

Down below the trail, overlooking Windermere, lies Dove Nest cottage; it was here that in 1830, a female poet, Felicia Dorothea Browne Hemans came to stay for the summer. She is renowned for her poetry, in particular one called *Casabianca*, better known as *The boy stood on the burning deck*.

A short way farther on from Jenkins Crag, when the trail forks, take the right branch and follow this as it bends downwards to cross a stream, after which it continues descending through woodland and eventually meets the head of a surfaced lane. Now press on down the lane, and when it comes down to a junction, just above the main road, turn right along a quieter road that eventually descends into the centre of Ambleside.

where she bred Herdwick sheep.

When you reach Troutbeck Post Office, leave the village road by branching right onto Robin Lane **B**, a surfaced track, although you may want to divert a little to visit Townend House farther down the road. Townend *(details of which can be found on page 95)* is an old slate and stone house that presents a unique insight into the life of a Lake District family through the centuries. Back on Robin Lane, when the surfacing ends, the lane continues as a rough track. At **C**, leave the main track by branching left through a kissing-gate onto a descending path for Skelghyll and Ambleside by Jenkins Crag, just after the track reaches its

Crinkle Crags

		GPS waypoints
Start	Great Langdale	 NY 286 061
Distance	7 miles (11.5km)	Ⓐ NY 271 053
Height gain	2,820 feet (860m)	Ⓑ NY 267 039
Approximate time	4 hours	Ⓒ NY 248 061
Parking	Old Dungeon Ghyll (Pay and Display)	
Route terrain	Rough and craggy mountain paths	
Ordnance Survey maps	Landranger 90 (Penrith & Keswick), Explorer OL6 (The English Lakes – South-western area)	

The traverse of Crinkle Crags, a switchback outing cavorting along an assortment of rocky bumps, is a classic Lakeland walk, combining interesting and rugged terrain that offers dramatic glimpses of the impressive east face of the mountain, and an airy, high-level walk with splendid views in all directions.

 The walk begins from the car park at Old Dungeon Ghyll, from which you walk out to the valley road and turn right to a junction across which lies the track to Stool End Farm. Pass between the farm buildings, and then keep ahead to locate the rough track that leads into Oxendale.

The path leads to a bridge Ⓐ spanning the river, and from it the way toils upwards across the lower slopes of Pike o'Blisco, and leads to a conspicuous knoll, Brown Howe, which offers an impressive view into the nearby Browney Gill.

Keep following the path upwards to a low depression between Pike o'Blisco and Cold Pike wherein reposes Red Tarn Ⓑ. Before reaching the tarn, however, turn right (west), crossing the stream flowing from the tarn, and following a rising path passing between Cold Pike and Great Knott. This last and minor summit is well worth a detour offering as it does the most splendid view across

SCALE 1:25 000 or 2½ INCHES to 1 MILE 4CM to 1KM

Great Cove to the craggy face of the Crinkles. The retrospective view of Pike o'Blisco and across Oxendale to the Langdale Pikes is quite impressive, too.

The main path leads up to the first crinkle, the south top, reached by a short rocky scramble. Here it is that the ridge of Crinkle Crags begins.

The continuation to the highest crinkle, Long Top, poses the only problem of the whole ascent, a feature known as the Bad Step. From the col between the first and second crinkles you can see a conspicuous gully, the natural way to go. But upward escape from the gully is barred by huge boulders. Walk up to just below these, and then take to the rock wall on the right, to ascend a short, rocky corner requiring just a few moves where hands are also needed as an aid to progress. The top of the crinkle lies by an easy path above the Bad Step. Walkers not overly happy about tackling the Bad Step need not fear that the summit is unavailable to them. From the col below all that is needed is a move to the left (west) to gain a narrow path, now well trodden, rising through a broad, shallow gully and placing you on Long Top just a short way from the summit.

What now remains is pure delight. The next dip is known as Mickle Door, and it leads on to the third crinkle before setting off for the fourth and fifth, the last of which is known as Gunson Knott.

This traverse of the ridge is marred only by the fact that it ends; it offers superb views of Bowfell, and numerous changes of terrain, direction, viewpoints, and nooks and crannies in

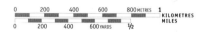

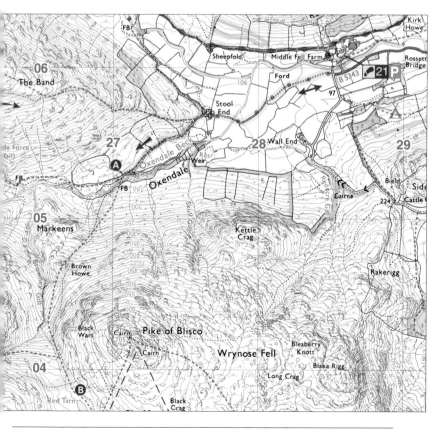

Crinkle Crags and Bowfell

which to shelter. Indeed, the very next 'crinkle', although it is set a little apart from the main fell, is called Shelter Crags. Beyond, the route drops rockily to the linking col with Bowfell, where lie the Three Tarns **C** offering a splendid view westwards of the Scafell groups of mountains.

All that remains is to locate the prominent path heading eastwards down the long ridge known as The Band, at the bottom of which you effect a return to Stool End Farm.

From Three Tarns there is an alternative way down, a little to the south of The Band, and descending into Buscoe Sike. This is steeper in places than The Band and leads past the ravine of Hell Gill to Whorneyside Force, an attractive waterfall. The way out then lies through Oxendale, joining the outward route before reaching Stool End Farm.

From the farm it is simply a question of retracing your steps to Old Dungeon Ghyll. ●

Pike o'Stickle and Stake Pass

Start	Great Langdale, New Dungeon Ghyll	**GPS waypoints**	
		🖉 NY 294 064	
Distance	6¼ miles (10km)	Ⓐ NY 291 066	
		Ⓑ NY 274 074	
Height gain	2,130 feet (650m)	Ⓒ NY 265 087	
Approximate time	4 hours	Ⓓ NY 261 074	
Parking	Stickle Ghyll car park (National Trust Pay and Display)		
Route terrain	Rough and steep fell country; some moorland		
Ordnance Survey maps	Landranger 90 (Penrith & Keswick), Explorer OL6 (The English Lakes – South-western area)		

Many walkers combine the upper reaches of this walk with those of the ascent of Harrison Stickle (Walk 14) to give a circular walk around the Pikes. But the present walk is bent on squeezing as much as possible out of these delectable fells, and perhaps in the process leading visitors to places they may not otherwise reach. One thing is certain: today's walkers will be treading in footprints more than 5,000 years old, since the hunter-gatherers of the Neolithic period settled down, became farmers and manufacturers of stone axes.

🖉 The walk sets off from the Stickle Ghyll car park by walking up to the left of the information shelter at the rear of

Pike o'Stickle and Loft Crag

the car park to access a brief, enclosed path that leads out to a junction of paths above Stickle Ghyll. Where the track divides, bear left and rise steadily along a stony path to a gate. Beyond,

Pike o'Stickle from The Band

the path divides again. Keep right, walking beside a wall to reach a tall stile and then drop down to cross Dungeon Ghyll **A**.

At this comparatively low point, Dungeon Ghyll seems little more than mildly interesting. But it was a popular visiting station for Victorian travellers, and before long becomes a dramatic ravine, blocked by a huge chockstone, and with a splendid waterfall.

Adventurous souls can venture into the ghyll, *but great care is needed, and there is no path of any substance.* Upwards the only way out involves scrambling. Those with a preference for survival will take the pitched and cairned path up Mark Gate, with a lovely, almost Alpine mountain pasture part way up that demands a pause to take in the scenery. Above, the pitched path continues its flight to higher ground overlooking Harrison Combe. Here, the path forks with one path going around the side of Loft Crag

towards Pike o'Stickle (Pike of Stickle on some maps), but on a clear day it is easy enough to scamper upwards onto Loft Crag and then follow the rocky ridge to the top of an impressive scree gully, the South Screes. Pike o'Stickle lies beyond and offers some very mild scrambling to reach its summit **B**. The view, as might be supposed, is remarkable.

The slopes below Pike o'Stickle are the site of a prehistoric axe factory, one that sent its axes throughout Britain and into Europe.

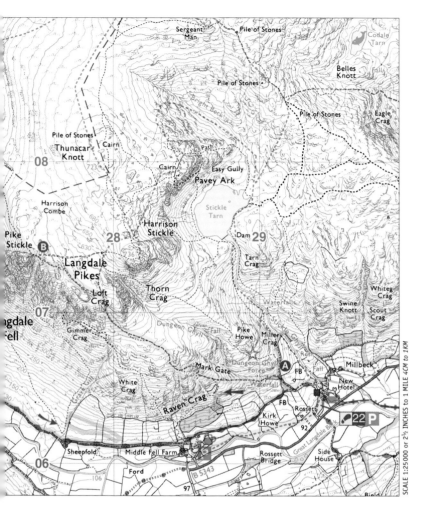

SCALE 1:25000 or 2½ INCHES to 1 MILE 4CM to 1KM

Equally remarkable is any descent from the top of Pike o'Stickle that does not retrace your steps to easier ground from whence a path heads out onto Martcrag Moor (for many years recorded on older maps as Martcrag Moo, which would hold rather more fascination were it not simply an error).

Martcrag Moor is often wet, and can be a bewildering place in poor visibility. But the target is the top of Stake Pass, where the Cumbria Way is encountered **C**. Although there are possible shortcuts, it is safest to keep following the path to the top of the pass, and there turning left.

Heading now south-west, the path traverses Langdale Combe beyond which it crosses Stake Gill and begins a steep descent to the valley below. As you descend it is easy to study the shape of the valley, Mickleden, and to see how it owes its origins to glacial action, having steep sides and clear hanging valleys.

Once in the valley bottom **D**, a broad track leads in a south-easterly and then easterly direction to Old Dungeon Ghyll. Here go through a gate and down to the car park. Turn right and walk out towards the valley road, but before reaching it go left on a signposted footpath that cuts across flat fields back to the start.

Troutbeck Valley

Start	Troutbeck	GPS waypoints
Distance	6 miles (9.5km); including The Tongue 7¾ miles (12.5km)	🖉 NY 412 027
Height gain	855 feet (260m); including The Tongue 1,330 feet (405m)	Ⓐ NY 417 027 Ⓑ NY 426 064 Ⓒ NY 421 054
Approximate time	3 hours; including The Tongue 4 hours	Ⓓ NY 416 039 Ⓔ NY 412 033
Parking	Church bridge	
Route terrain	Rough fell tracks and lanes	
Ordnance Survey maps	Landranger 90 (Penrith & Keswick), Explorer OL7 (The English Lakes – South-eastern area)	

The valley of Troutbeck probes a slender finger northwards from Windermere shore towards the smooth-sided fells of Kentmere and Caudale Moor. This is an ancient through-route over the Kirkstone Pass and into Patterdale and as such few visitors stop to explore the dale. This walk invites such exploration, making a simple tour of the valley, and visiting the largest farm owned by Beatrix Potter. An extension offers the opportunity to 'bag' The Tongue, a small but significant summit at the head of the valley. Since 1980, Troutbeck has been a conservation area, and those who appreciate vernacular architecture will delight in what the valley has to offer.

🖉 From the parking area, turn right to cross the footbridge beside Church Bridge, and walk alongside the road for

Jesus Church, Troutbeck

about 100 yds. Cross the road and head up the stony track opposite. Follow the track as it climbs steadily upwards, and continues easily, later merging with another coming in from the right. Just after this junction Ⓐ, the track forks. Bear left down to a gate, and take a now descending path that runs across the fell slopes above Limefitt Park, with The Tongue and the upper Troutbeck Valley now in view ahead.

Keep on past Long Green Head Farm, and stay with the ongoing track beyond, which is perfectly clear and presses on steadily, but gradually slims down to a footpath as it heads into the recesses of Hagg Gill between The Tongue and the smooth-sided Kentmere fells.

At a gate, just level with the southern end of The Tongue, it is possible to shortcut the walk a little by going through the gate, turning immediately left through another gate and then heading down to a footbridge across Hagg Gill, beyond which you ascend to the return track on the opposite side.

To extend the walk a little, simply keep on the original path, which takes you farther into Hagg Gill. Stay with the track as far as a footbridge spanning the gill, close by a stone barn. Cross the bridge and walk up to a gate **B** where you join the return track, now heading south to a gate where those who went up The Tongue will rejoin the route – see over.

(Strong walkers wanting to make more of the day can turn right on reaching the track, and follow it northwards for about 1 mile until, just before you encounter a wall, you can swing left to climb onto the northern end of The Tongue. There is a quad bike track and a path, but neither is especially necessary. Once on the ridge, a grassy path runs all the way south to the fine cairn on the summit of the fell. Beyond this a steep path goes down to a lower 'summit', and on down again until you cross a fence by a step-stile, after which the path gradually swings down to the left to rejoin the main path below. This is a lovely extension, and should be included in the walk if possible.)

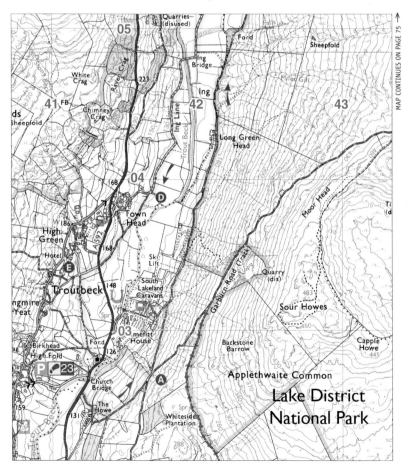

MAP CONTINUES ON PAGE 75 →

The Tongue

Continue with the main track, which shortly starts to descend, until you reach a wall corner. A few strides farther on, leave the main track by going through a kissing-gate on the left onto a path for Troutbeck village. This takes you down across a sloping grassy pasture, keeping to the left of Hall Hill, a large grassy mound.

This area is Troutbeck Park, linked to the nearby farm, one that has always been a large sheep farm. In 1923, the farm came up for sale, and was under threat of development. However, Beatrix Potter, who for the previous ten years had observed the functions of the dutiful wife of a country solicitor, living at Near Sawrey, decided to buy the farm. Three years after she bought it, she decided to run the farm herself with the aid of George Walker, shepherd brother-in-law of Tom Storey, who ran Hill Top Farm in Sawrey. Together, Walker and Potter built up a celebrated flock of Herdwick sheep, a small and hardy breed indigenous to the Lake District. When she died in 1943, Beatrix Potter left 14 farms and 4,000 acres of land to the National Trust.

The descending path reaches the farm access at Hagg Bridge **C**, and thereafter follows a surfaced route to Ing Bridge and onward towards Troutbeck village. Later, when the lane turns right to go up to Town Head, leave it by branching left onto a bridleway **D** between walls. The bridleway comes out to meet the valley road. Cross, and go into the lane opposite that leads up to Troutbeck.

When the lane swings to the right **E**, leave it by branching left onto a path for the church. When confronted by two gates, take that on the right, passing through a kissing-gate to follow the ongoing path beside a wall. Shortly the path narrows and runs down between fences. The path is straightforward and leads down to intercept a broad track. Turn left along the side of the graveyard and walk out to the road, there turning right to walk the short distance back to Church Bridge to complete the walk.

The origins of Troutbeck's church are lost, but it certainly existed in the 16th century. In the *Records relating to the Barony of Kendale,* it is recorded on 18 July 1562: 'Whereas Troutbeck is distant and remote from the parish church of St Martin's Windermere, the space of three myles soe that they cann neither bring the bodyes of the dead to be buryed att their parish church without their great and extraordinary cost and discommoditye nor carrye

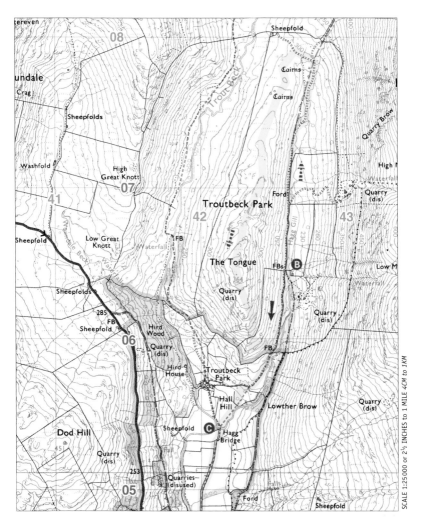

SCALE 1:25000 or 2½ INCHES to 1 MILE 4CM to 1KM

their children to be baptized without great danger of soul and bodye, nor can they by any means come to hear Divine Service, to receive the Sacrament nor to be instructed in the word of God as becometh Christians, without their so great cost, travel, danger and incommodity, William Downham, Bp. of Chester, licenced the newly rebuilt Chapel of Jesus at Troutbeck for the celebration of the Sacraments etc., with the consent "of that worshipful man Mr Adam Carehouse", rector of Windermere'.

The key aspects of this record are that in 1562, the chapel was 'newly rebuilt', clearly implying that a chapel existed at an earlier date.

The present church was dismantled and rebuilt in 1736, allegedly on the site of a 15th-century chapel. Major restoration was carried out by the Victorians in 1861, and much of the church now displays work of the Arts and Crafts Movement, notably that of Edward Burne-Jones and William Morris. Unusually, the church is not dedicated to a saint, but is known simply as Jesus Church.

Scout Scar and Cunswick Fell

Start	Kendal	GPS waypoints
Distance	9 miles (14.5km)	📖 SD 516 922
Height gain	1,100 feet (335m)	Ⓐ SD 508 907
		Ⓑ SD 502 917
Approximate time	4 hours	Ⓒ SD 489 924
Parking	Short stay car park at the southern end of town, or Abbot Hall car park (Pay and Display)	Ⓓ SD 491 943
Route terrain	Generally easy; good paths or tracks throughout	
Ordnance Survey maps	Landranger 97 (Kendal & Morecambe), Explorer OL7 (The English Lakes – South-eastern area)	

The limestone scars that present their posterior to Kendal are not so obvious to those who follow the dual carriageway around the town. But they are dramatic and well worth visiting. This walk, however, opts to make a start in the company of the River Kent, before heading onto the scars.

📖 Begin by heading past the Abbot Hall Art Gallery and Museum at the southern end of Kendal to reach the path alongside the River Kent. Turn right along the riverbank on a path that leads out to meet the main road at a busy junction. Cross with care into Milnthorpe Road, and then take the first turning on the left (South Road). Keep following the river, soon joining a riverside path once more, which leads round to the end of Romney Gardens. Go left and cross into Ford Terrace, and immediately resume a riverside path, following it as it passes water treatment works, just after which the river changes direction.

Stay along the riverbank, keeping an eye open for goosander, mallard, moorhen, coot and an occasional goldeneye, and keep following the path round a bend, and then climb up steps beside a wall. Bear left into Scroggs Wood, a Woodland Trust property. Go through the woods, emerging on the other side to meet a surfaced lane. Turn right, and follow the lane out to meet the A6 Ⓐ.

Go left, crossing the road with care, and after about 45 yds, leave the A6 by branching right on a signposted path for Helsington Laithes. At the end of a row of cottages, turn right (sign-posted for Helsington Laithes Manor), almost immediately passing the entrance to the manor, and then going forward between large gate pillars onto a broad track between moss-covered walls. The track leads up to an under-pass below the A591. On the other side, the ongoing track climbs to meet a surfaced lane. At Lane Head, bear right through a metal gate onto a stony field track climbing into pasture.

A short way on, the track forks. Keep left and almost immediately, as the track forks again, branch right to a wall corner, and then keep alongside a wall (on your right), and, on approaching a white bungalow, bear across to a gated gap-stile in a wall corner, giving onto a narrow road (Brigsteer Road). Turn right, taking care against approaching traffic, for almost 500 yds, as far as a signposted path on the left for Scout Scar

and Barrow Field, immediately adjoining a milestone dating from 1900 **B**.

Cross a stile here, and bear diagonally left towards wooded Scout Scar, crossing Kendal racecourse, and here entering the Lake District National Park. Follow a broad, grassy track, striking left eventually to meet a metal kissing-gate in a wall below Scout Scar. Keep forward on the limestone path beyond, between gorse and holly. The path crosses another wall and later becomes soft, springy turf, a delight to walk on, with improving views to the east over Kendal.

Maintain the same direction, ignoring branching paths, and follow the track up to its highest point, crossing just to the south of a large cairn to reach a path *on the very edge of Scout Scar – no place to let children or dogs run freely*. Turn right, following the edge of the scar to reach a mushroom-shaped shelter from which there is a fine view in all directions, embracing the Yorkshire Dales, the Forest of Bowland, Morecambe Bay, and the central Lakeland fells. The shelter was built in 1912 to commemorate the coronation of King George V.

Continue past the shelter, still following a broad path above Scout Scar. Eventually, this is deflected to the right, as it descends to meet a road (Underbarrow Road). At the road, turn right, passing the entrance to a car park, and just after this, branch left onto a narrow path through light woodland, soon to meet a service track for a nearby radio mast **C**.

Bear left passing the radio mast, following a path that leads to a kissing-gate in a wall corner. Through this, go forward on either of two grassy tracks (signposted to Cunswick Fell). For a while, the path runs alongside a wall, and then from a wall corner (signpost), bear left on a grassy track, leading across towards Cunswick Fell.

Continue to follow the wallside path,

which leads steadily on to the top of Cunswick Fell. After you break free from the wall, continue on an obvious path to the summit of the fell, marked by a large cairn **D**.

From the cairn, about face, backtracking a little, but look for a clear grassy path veering left, away from the outward route, that descends to locate a gap-stile at a wall corner. Through this go forward alongside a wall, but then bearing away from the wall to continue following a green path across pasture towards the rise of Kendal Fell ahead.

A couple of stiles give onto a footbridge spanning the A591. On the other side, go forward on a gently rising green path onto Kendal Fell, and keep following the path, which leads up into the edge of Kendal Golf Course, reaching it at a wall corner. The path across the golf course is waymarked, and near a bench the path divides. Keep forward, passing the bench and soon heading downhill towards Kendal.

The path descends to a gap at a wall corner, and then continues beyond past another bench with a fine view across the Kent Valley. As soon as you can safely do so, drop down to a track below which runs along the valley intake wall. Turn right along this to the head of a surfaced lane, and now follow the lane towards Kendal.

Go down to meet a road, and there turn right (Queens Road). At its end, keep forward and then shortly bear right towards Tenterfell Court. Keep following the main road (signposted for Underbarrow and Brigsteer). Go down High Tenterfell to a road junction, and there head straight across into Bankfield Road. Pass the Brigsteer turning, and go into Gillinggate, and then continue down to meet the main Kendal street. Here, cross the road at a pedestrian crossing and turn right to return to the car park starting point. ●

Far Easedale and Helm Crag

		GPS waypoints
Start	Mill Bridge, north of Grasmere	📷 NY 336 091
Distance	8¾ miles (14km)	Ⓐ NY 332 081
Height gain	2,200 feet (670m)	Ⓑ NY 318 094
Approximate time	4½ hours	Ⓒ NY 295 102
Parking	Limited roadside parking on main road	
Route terrain	*Rugged going with numerous undulations, and rough conditions underfoot*	
Ordnance Survey maps	Landranger 90 (Penrith & Keswick), Explorers OL6 (The English Lakes – South-western area) and OL7 (The English Lakes – South-eastern area)	

Within minutes you can be away from the clamour of Grasmere and striding up Far Easdale, to all intents and purposes miles from anywhere. The farther you penetrate the dale, following an ancient packhorse trail that crossed the fells into Borrowdale, the more beautifully desolate it becomes. Helm Crag lords it over the dale to the north, and, while normally ascended early in the day, is here left until the very end, the walk preferring to amble up Far Easedale, gaining height gradually, before romping back along the lovely ridge that ends at Helm Crag.

📷 The usual start is from the village of Grasmere itself, setting off along Easedale Road to Goody Bridge. But there is a variant start from farther north along the valley road, at Mill Bridge, where the Northern Coast-to-Coast Walk crosses. This alternative start shuns the bustle of Grasmere, delightful though it is, in exchange for lovely views of the lush farmland north of the village and the rise of fellside to culminate in Fairfield, Seat Sandal and the Helvellyn range.

Turn down the side road at Mill Bridge, soon passing the Old Mill Cottage, and continuing to Low Mill Bridge, a small hump-backed bridge spanning the River Rothay. Here turn left, still following a narrow lane, one

that eventually leads past the turning to Thorney How Youth Hostel and in due course meets a T-junction at Goody Bridge Ⓐ. On the way, the road gains a little height above the valley, and offers lovely views of the farmland and fells of Fairfield in particular. Throughout this section, Helm Crag rises steeply to its craggy summit, though nothing is seen from this angle of the rock figures that have become known as 'The Lion and the Lamb'.

At the T-junction, turn right to pass Goody Bridge Farm. Keep following the road, passing the footbridge that takes walkers to Easedale Tarn. Stay along the road (signed for Far Easedale), which soon bends left and crosses a wide, open area of grassland.

Over on the left-hand side of the dale, small farm buildings sit tight against the fells for protection. Some were once the home of the Greene family, far-from-affluent statesmen farmers who died in a snowstorm while returning from a sale in Langdale. Unable to find their way home, the two parents lived out their final moments in the storm. Meanwhile, their eldest daughter, Sally, no more than a child herself, took charge of her siblings, tended the fire, milked the cows and pressed on with the work of their farm until the storm abated. Once the alarm was raised, their dead parents were soon found on the ridge above Blindtarn Moss.

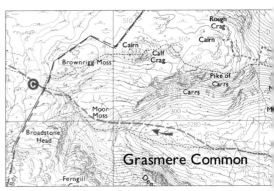

Continue past Little Parrock cottage, and, when the lane forks, branch right onto a bridleway, a stony track. A short way farther on when this forks, branch left, soon joining the company of Far Easedale Gill. A clear path now leads on into the dale to reach a footbridge at Stythwaite Steps **B** – 'Stythwaite' being the old name for the lower part of the valley.

In Far Easedale

Over the footbridge, and a short way farther, ignore a tempting waymark above (which leads up to Easedale Tarn), and instead branch right onto a narrow path that continues the route up the valley.

The path now rises steadily, at varying distances from the gill, until, near the head of the dale, the path rises more steeply, following a constructed path to reach the remains of an old fenceline on a col, which marks the parish boundary **C**. Beyond lies the grassy gulf of upper Wythburn, and a narrow route across to Greenup Edge.

But this walk turns round at the fenceline, and takes a clear path, rising gently in an easterly direction to pass Calf Crag, and so begin a delightful, undulating course along one of the finest, and possibly most neglected ridges, in Lakeland. With a deal of switching about, the path teases a route from the crags, generally descending towards Gibson Knott. There is a dominant path, but this is fragmented and easily missed. But the general direction is rarely in doubt. Just keep heading for Helm Crag, and make the most of this splendid traverse. To the north

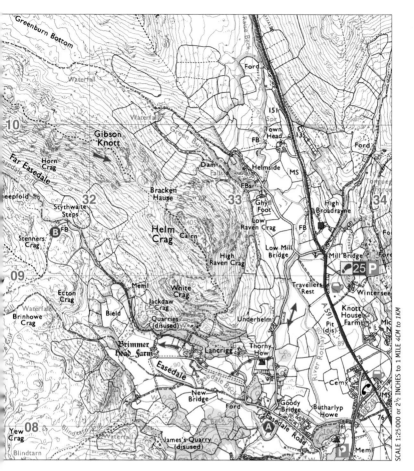

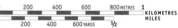

SCALE 1:25 000 or 2½ INCHES to 1 MILE 4CM to 1KM

lies Greenburndale, a remote, grassy valley with few visitors, even though a pathway runs up its length and onto Calf Crag. North of that, Steel Fell takes on an increasingly shapely profile, its steep, rarely visited slopes falling to Dunmail Raise.

A final pull leads onto the surprisingly rocky summit of Helm Crag. Bold folk may venture up the rocky upthrust to touch the very top. Sensible folk will sit and watch them do it. Across the valley rises Fairfield, with Helvellyn farther north. To the south, rising above Grasmere is Loughrigg Fell.

A clear path leads across the summit, and soon brings into view the rocks that make 'The Lion and the Lamb', still discernible as such. Keep on along the

path, soon descending quite steeply and requiring careful placement of feet. Lower down a broad grassy path appears on the right, and this is the way to go. It appears to be going the wrong way, heading back into Far Easedale. But it is correct, and later is seen to sweep round to the left to face towards Grasmere. Keep following this down (even up at one point!), and eventually it drops to meet a wall in the valley bottom. Go right for a short distance, as far as a clear walled gap on the left, through which the outward route is soon rejoined, and should be followed back to the start.

The Langdale valleys

		GPS waypoints	
Start	Great Langdale, New Dungeon Ghyll	✎	NY 294 064
Distance	8½ miles (13.5km)	Ⓐ	NY 289 051
Height gain	1,690 feet (515m)	Ⓑ	NY 300 032
Approximate time	4½ hours	Ⓒ	NY 312 029
Parking	Stickle Ghyll car park (National Trust Pay and Display)	Ⓓ	NY 321 041
		Ⓔ	NY 308 057
Route terrain	Rough fell paths; woodland; some road walking		
Ordnance Survey maps	Landranger 90 (Penrith & Keswick), Explorers OL6 (The English Lakes – South-western area) and OL7 (The English Lakes – South-eastern area)		

The two Langdale valleys – Great and Little – are separated by the craggy bulk of Lingmoor Fell, and combining them offers a succession of fine views. The Langdale Pikes dominate much of the first part of the walk, along with the headwall of Great Langdale in the form of Crinkle Crags and Bowfell. But once you pass into Little Langdale it is the Coniston Fells, notably Wetherlam and Swirl How that ease into view; that they are seen from an unusual angle makes them all the more interesting.

✎ The walk begins from the Stickle Ghyll car park in Great Langdale by walking up to the left of the buildings at the rear of the car park to access a brief, enclosed path that soon leads out to a junction of paths at Stickle Ghyll. Where the track divides, bear left and rise steadily to a gate. Beyond, the path divides again. Keep left again, now descending to cross a footbridge.

Almost immediately you encounter a feature known as the Ring Garth, a circle of great walls around the valley enclosing the arable land in the valley bottom. The garth, which can still be traced around most of the valley, takes the form of the stone wall on your right, which is composed of a higher incidence of large and in situ boulders than the comparatively juvenile wall on

your left. This distinction becomes more evident the farther along the valley you travel, and it hallmarks the time of Norse settlement after the 10th century. Certainly the ring garth was in place by the early 13th century, when a document refers to the 'inclosed land of Great Langden' under which it was granted to Conishead Priory.

The first evidence of human activity in Langdale, however, is associated with Neolithic axe factories on the high slopes of the Langdale Pikes, which are thought to have been in use from around 6,000 years ago. What makes these axe factories particularly noteworthy is that they mark a change of lifestyle among our prehistoric ancestors from hunter-gatherers, always on the move, to a more settled period when static farming in the valleys freed the axe makers from the necessities of the hunt.

When you reach Old Dungeon Ghyll, the first of the properties in Langdale acquired by the National Trust, in 1929, go through a gate and follow the track down to the car park. Bear right along the car park access to meet a surfaced lane. Go left over a road bridge spanning Great Langdale Beck to a T-junction. Turn right to another junction, and there turn left, walking along the road, but only as far as the entrance to a campsite on the left, next to a fine specimen of a pollarded ash tree.

Go into the campsite, on a footpath for Side Pike and Lingmoor Fell. Follow the right-hand wall to cross a footbridge, and then leave the site as the path begins to climb the fellside above. After a narrow pasture you enter a small larch plantation. Climb through the plantation, leaving it at a gate to press on steeply beside a wall. Eventually the track levels as it moves on to a ladder-stile over which you join the road **Ⓐ**, linking the two Langdale valleys, and with Blea Tarn now suddenly coming into view.

Cross the road and walk with a wall on your left to a gate through which the lovely path to Blea Tarn begins. Follow the path beyond Blea Tarn, and when it divides, ignore the footbridge on the left, and bear right to gate/wall giving out onto the great expanse of Blea Moss. Now descend alongside Bleamoss Beck, the path later running parallel with a wall. But when the wall changes direction, bear off to the right, continuing with the main path that runs out to meet the Wrynose Pass road. As you approach the road, the path sinks

Little Langdale Beck at Slater Bridge

into marshy ground, but without any detriment to route finding.

On reaching the road, turn left and follow it down to Fell Foot Farm. On the way you pass two notable features: one, the evident volcanic upthrust of Castle Howe, site of a Neolithic hill fort, the other (accessed by a gate just above Fell Foot) known as a Ting Mound.

The Ting Mound, sometimes Thing Mound, or Thing Moot, is an open-air court, meeting place, or parliament, used by those responsible for the administration of the countryside. Generally, they appear to date from the 7th-9th centuries, and some are recorded in the *Domesday Book*, suggesting a continuing use into the medieval period.

Fell Foot Farm is also interesting. Dating from the 17th century, this was originally a coaching inn, reputedly used as a hideaway for illicit goods smuggled over the fells. Beatrix Potter

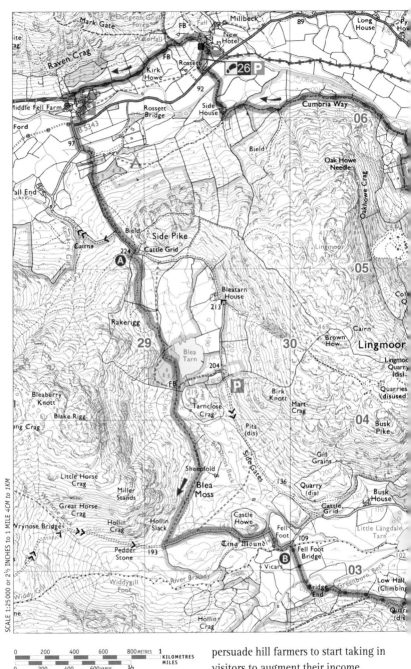

SCALE 1:25000 or 2½ INCHES to 1 MILE 4CM to 1KM

```
0     200    400    600    800 METRES    1
                                         KILOMETRES
                                         MILES
0     200    400    600 YARDS     ½
```

was responsible for reviving the fortunes of Fell Foot as a place of accommodation and hospitality when, while working as a land agent for the National Trust, she did much to

persuade hill farmers to start taking in visitors to augment their income.

Stay along the road after leaving Fell Foot Farm until you reach Fell Foot Bridge **B** on the right, which spans the infant River Brathay. Cross this and now take to a broad track across flat pastures to reach another neat bridge beside a

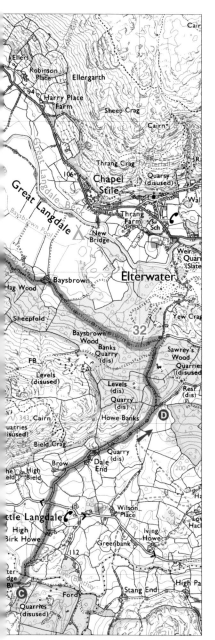

lies a short way farther on beyond an area of slate spoil, a reminder that this is mining country. After the cottages, the track levels as it leads on to a gate on the left **C** giving onto Slater Bridge, a typical packhorse bridge spanning the Brathay *(see Walk 11 for more information)*.

Beyond the bridge, follow an ascending path beside a wall that eventually leads up to High Birk Howe Farm. Turn left and follow the farm access out to a lane. Turn left and immediately right into a side lane leading up to Dale Head, after which the road surfacing ends and the ongoing track becomes stony and uneven.

Just after a gate the track forks **D**, with the main track continuing its descent to Elterwater. Bear left at this point, ascending easily into woodland and passing what might be called a 'Money Tree' – it's self-evident when you find it.

Following a short ascent the path descends between luxurious moss-covered walls. Keep following the track until you reach a cottage and a narrow surfaced lane. Turn left here, and now follow the lane through delightful light woodland to reach Baysbrown Farm. There continue along the bridleway for Oak Howe.

Shortly, when the track forks, keep left, and at the next divide, go right. Another splendid path takes you on through the woodland, and then down to the group of buildings at Oak Howe **E**. At a signpost turn left for New Dungeon Ghyll. The ongoing path is straight-forward and provides fine views of the Langdale Pikes and the head of Langdale. Continue with the path on a clear and obvious route to Side House Farm.

Now all that remains is to follow the farm access out to the main valley road, which you join close by the starting point. ●

cottage, spanning Greenburn Beck.

Beyond the cottage the track rises gently across a fell shoulder. High above Little Langdale Tarn, the track forks. Here branch left heading down to a walled track that passes High Hallgarth cottage, a 17th-century stone-built structure. Low Hall Garth

Scandale

		GPS waypoints
Start	Ambleside	📝 NY 377 044
Distance	8¾ miles (14km)	**Ⓐ** NY 376 062
Height gain	2,625 feet (800m)	**Ⓑ** NY 374 098
Approximate time	5 hours	**Ⓒ** NY 388 096
Parking	Ambleside	
Route terrain	Rough and rocky fell country; minor roads	
Ordnance Survey maps	Landranger 90 (Penrith & Keswick), Explorer OL7 (The English Lakes – South-eastern area)	

Scandale is for connoisseurs, a glorious, infrequently visited dale probing northwards from Ambleside, and an ancient thoroughfare into Patterdale. For every walker who ventures into Scandale, there will be a thousand or more on the long ridge to the west. It is easy to see why; the ridge is part of the Fairfield Horseshoe, Scandale is not, and all the better for it: undemonstrative, a placid dale wherein the sensitive walker might stride an easy day and return mightily refreshed.

The present walk, is a compromise, using the ridge to gain height above Scandale before effecting a simple return.

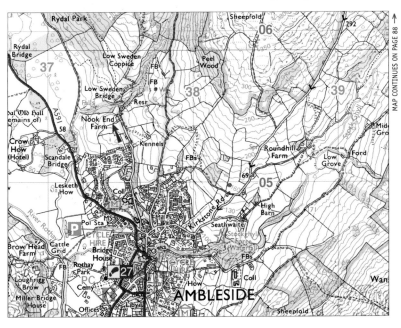

Begin from the market cross in Ambleside, and set off up North Road. When you reach the top of Smithy Brow, near the **Golden Rule inn**, turn left past the pub, and shortly turn right into Nook Lane. Follow the lane as far as Nook End Farm, passing through the farmyard, and then taking the left-hand track beyond, quickly reaching Low Sweden Bridge. Once over the bridge, the path goes to the left then curls back on itself as it heads up to a gap at a wall corner.

The Langdale Pikes from the track up to High Sweden Bridge

The ascending track is clear and straightforward and leads up to another wall gap after which, with the main path keeping to the right, a second path can be seen ascending towards a wall on the left Ⓐ. Go this way, and soon cross a ladder-stile. The ongoing wall is a feat of considerable ingenuity and a testament to the Lakeland wall builders of old. The way upwards runs roughly parallel with it, passing first Low Pike and then continuing to High Pike. Already there is a fine sense of openness about the ridge, with occasional glimpses down into Scandale and across to Red Screes.

Terminus of this ridge walk is Dove Crag, a fairly innocuous summit that belies the fiercesome cliffs to the north east, overlooking Dovedale.

From Dove Crag the way lies down to Little Hart Crag and the head of Scandale. *Walkers wanting to take a variant route can omit Dove Crag altogether and opt for a path that descends from the main ridge Ⓑ a little earlier, roughly in an easterly direction, to the fine-cairned High Bakestones, and then down to pass to the south of Little Hart Crag to Scandale Pass.*

Otherwise, from Dove Crag, backtrack a little to locate the remains of a fenceline dropping eastwards towards Little Hart Crag. The going is not the easiest, but you can seek out the gentlest line; nor is what remains of the fenceline especially critical to route finding, although it does help in poor visibility.

Little Hart Crag lies in a no-man's land between Dove Crag (not nearby Hart Crag, as might be expected) to the west and Red Screes to the east. It is the culmination of a long, curving ridge, High Hartsop Dodd, which rises from the low ground south of Brothers Water in Patterdale. Topped by two craggy beetling brows, Little Hart Crag is a fine place to wile away a few hours on a warm summer's day, letting the world slip by largely unnoticed.

Scandale Pass Ⓒ lies due south of Little Hart Crag, and a ladder-stile there gives onto the ancient bridleway that runs the length of the dale, eventually, after two long and lovely miles, passing High Sweden Bridge beyond which it enters woodland for a while. After the woodland, the descending track is enclosed between walls and leads unerringly down into Ambleside, eventually reaching the top of Smithy Brow, with only the brief North Road to complete the walk. ●

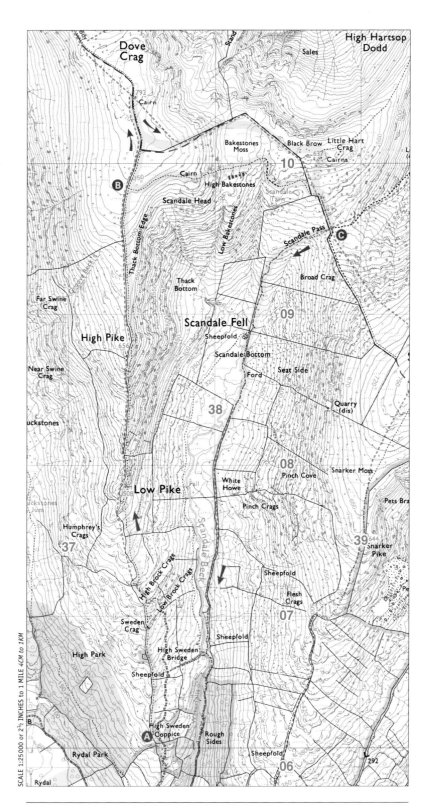

SCALE 1:25 000 or 2½ INCHES to 1 MILE 4CM to 1KM

High Hartsop
Dodd

Dove
Crag

Sales

Cairn

Bakestones
Moss

Black Brow

Little Hart
Crag

10

Cairns

B

Cairn

High Bakestones

Scandale
Tarn

Scandale Head

C

Thack Bottom Edge

Low Bakestones

Scandale Pass

Far Swine
Crag

High Pike

Thack
Bottom

Broad Crag

09

Scandale Fell

Near Swine
Crag

Sheepfold

Scandale Bottom

Seat Side

uckstones

Ford

38

Quarry
(dis)

08

Pinch Cove

Snarker Moss

Low Pike

White
Howe

Pets Bra

uckstones
um

Pinch Crags

Humphrey's
Crags

39

Snarker
Pike

37

High Brock Crags

Low Brock Crags

Scandale Beck

Sheepfold

Flesh
Crags

07

Pe

Sweden
Crag

High Sweden
Bridge

Sheepfold

High Park

Sheepfold

Sheepfold

A

High Sweden
Coppice

Rough
Sides

Sheepfold

B

Rydal Park

292

Rydal

Bowfell

		GPS waypoints	
Start	Great Langdale	🚶	NY 286 061
Distance	7½ miles (12km)	**A**	NY 276 057
Height gain	2,855 feet (870)	**B**	NY 248 060
Approximate time	4½ hours	**C**	NY 240 072
Parking	Old Dungeon Ghyll	**D**	NY 247 075
Route terrain	Rough mountain fell tracks; *not advised in poor visibility*	**E**	NY 261 074
Ordnance Survey maps	Landranger 90 (Penrith & Keswick), Explorer OL6 (The English Lakes – South-western area)		

All the high fells of Langdale are popular; Bowfell, being the highest, is in consequence an experience you will have to share with someone else. But it is a huge fell, and there is plenty of room in which to lose yourself, which is an excellent reason for not attempting Bowfell in anything other than clear conditions. *With Bowfell it is not height that is the draw, but rather the long approach via The Band, the ascent of rocky slopes, the exploration of the trek across towards Esk Pike, the final, long walk out down Rossett Gill and through delectable Mickleden, and, of course, the stunning views.*

🚶 Walk out from the Old Dungeon Ghyll car park to cross a bridge and reach the valley road. Turn right to a point where the road changes direction, and here leave the road and walk ahead onto the broad farm access leading to Stool End.

Pass between the farm buildings to gain the open fellside. Ignore the track branching off to the right into Mickleden, and turn briefly towards Oxendale, then look for a clear and substantially renovated path **A** setting off up The Band. The path rises to a wall and kissing-gate from where there is a fine view of Pike of Stickle and its immense scree run.

The route up The Band generally keeps to the Oxendale side, but occasionally wanders over to take a peek into Mickleden. Towards the top, and just after Bowfell comes into view, you reach a grassy plateau. Beyond that, the trail continues an uneventful rise to the col between Bowfell and Crinkle Crags, wherein lie the Three Tarns **B**. The crags of Bowfell Links are especially prominent now, as, too, are the highest summits of England, Scafell Pike and Scafell, seen off to the west across the vast boggy bowl known as Great Moss.

From the col a rough stony ascent brings you to the top of Bowfell. Bowfell was described in 1902, by F.G. Brabant in *The English Lakes* as '... conspicuous among the lake mountains for its graceful, tapering peak ... It is a wild and rocky, though not very precipitous mountain, and the confused

Wall End Farm, Langdale Pikes and Mickleden

way in which its top is strewn with rock-masses is only equalled by Scafell Pikes. Few of the lake mountains are better worth ascending'.

The speediest and surest return to Langdale is back the way you came, but to continue the walk, leave the summit in a northerly direction taking a cairned

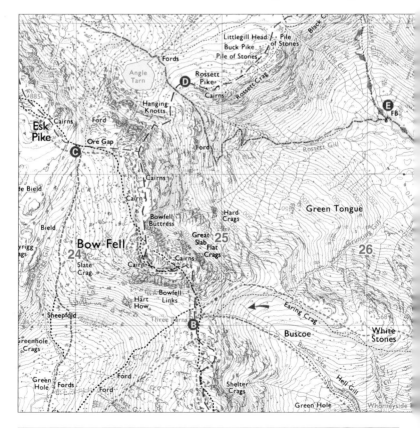

crags of Esk Pike, aiming to the west of Angle Tarn, around which a path circles to intercept a much more substantial track below Tongue Head, an ancient route across the fells and more than likely the way stone axes manufactured on Langdale's slopes were taken out to the coast.

From Angle Tarn, beautifully set against the crags of Hanging Knotts, the path rises a little as it heads for a gap 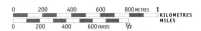 to the south of Rossett Pike. Beyond, a much-restored path zigzags into the head of Mickleden, slipping downwards to meet the Cumbria Way at a wooden footbridge **E** at the foot of the Stake Pass. Now all that remains is to follow a straightforward route in a south-easterly direction back to Old Dungeon Ghyll. ●

and steadily descending route to another col, Ore Gap **C**. *Pay close attention to the route to Ore Gap as it is easy to wander off line.*

From the col descend beneath the

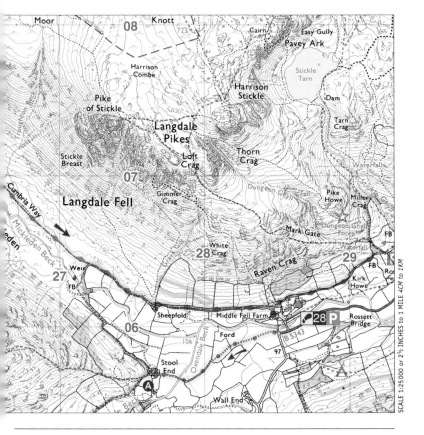

Further Information

Safety on the Hills

The hills, mountains and moorlands of Britain, though of modest height compared with those in many other countries, need to be treated with respect. Friendly and inviting in good weather, they can quickly be transformed into wet, misty, windswept and potentially dangerous areas of wilderness in bad weather. Even on an outwardly fine and settled summer day, conditions can rapidly deteriorate at high altitudes and, in winter, even more so.

Therefore it is advisable to always take both warm and waterproof clothing, sufficient nourishing food, a hot drink, first-aid kit, torch and whistle. Wear suitable footwear, such as strong walking-boots or shoes that give a good grip over rocky terrain and on slippery slopes. Try to obtain a local weather forecast and bear it in mind before you start. Do not be afraid to abandon your proposed route and return to your starting point in the event of a sudden and unexpected deterioration in the weather. Do not go alone and allow enough time to finish the walk well before nightfall.

Most of the walks described in this book do not venture into remote wilderness areas and will be safe to do, given due care and respect, at any time of year in all but the most unreasonable weather. Indeed, a crisp, fine winter day often provides perfect walking conditions, with firm ground underfoot and a clarity that is not possible to achieve in the other seasons of the year. A few walks, however, are suitable only for reasonably fit and experienced hill walkers able to use a compass and should definitely not be tackled by anyone else during the winter months or in bad weather, especially high winds and mist. These are indicated in the general description that precedes each of the walks.

Walkers and the Law

The Countryside and Rights of Way Act (CRoW Act 2000) extends the rights of access previously enjoyed by walkers in England and Wales. Implementation of these rights began on 19 September 2004. The Act amends existing legislation and for the first time provides access on foot to certain types of land – defined as mountain, moor, heath, down and registered common land.

Where You Can Go
Rights of Way
Prior to the introduction of the CRoW Act, walkers could only legally access the countryside along public rights of way. These are either 'footpaths' (for walkers only) or 'bridleways' (for walkers, riders on horseback and pedal cyclists). A third category called 'Byways open to all traffic' (BOATs), is used by motorised vehicles as well as those using non-mechanised transport. Mainly they are green lanes, farm and estate roads, although occasionally they will be found crossing mountainous area.

Rights of way are marked on Ordnance Survey maps. Look for the green broken lines on the Explorer maps, or the red dashed lines on Landranger maps.

The term 'right of way' means exactly what it says. It gives a right of passage over what, for the most part, is private land. Under pre-CRoW legislation walkers were required to keep to the line of the right of way and not stray onto land on either side. If you did inadvertently wander off the right of way, either because of faulty map reading or because the route was not clearly indicated on the ground, you were technically trespassing.

Local authorities have a legal obligation to ensure that rights of way are kept clear and free of obstruction, and are signposted where they leave metalled roads. The duty of local authorities to install signposts extends to the placing of signs along a path or way, but only where the authority considers it necessary to have a signpost or waymark to assist persons unfamiliar with the locality.

Countryside Access Charter

Your rights of way are:

- public footpaths – on foot only. Sometimes waymarked in yellow
- bridleways – on foot, horseback and pedal cycle. Sometimes waymarked in blue
- byways (usually old roads), most 'roads used as public paths' and, of course, public roads – all traffic has the right of way

Use maps, signs and waymarks to check rights of way. Ordnance Survey Explorer and Landranger maps show most public rights of way

On rights of way you can:

- take a pram, pushchair or wheelchair if practicable
- take a dog (on a lead or under close control)
- take a short route round an illegal obstruction or remove it sufficiently to get past

You have a right to go for recreation to:

- public parks and open spaces – on foot
- most commons near older towns and cities – on foot and sometimes on horseback
- private land where the owner has a formal agreement with the local authority

In addition you can use the following by local or established custom or consent, but ask for advice if you are unsure:

- many areas of open country, such as moorland, fell and coastal areas, especially those in the care of the National Trust, and some commons
- some woods and forests, especially those owned by the Forestry Commission
- country parks and picnic sites
- most beaches
- canal towpaths
- some private paths and tracks Consent sometimes extends to horse-riding and cycling

For your information:

- county councils and London boroughs maintain and record rights of way, and register commons
- obstructions, dangerous animals, harassment and misleading signs on rights of way are illegal and you should report them to the county council
- paths across fields can be ploughed, but must normally be reinstated within two weeks
- landowners can require you to leave land to which you have no right of access
- motor vehicles are normally permitted only on roads, byways and some 'roads used as public paths'

Further Information

The New Access Rights

Access Land

As well as being able to walk on existing rights of way, under the new legislation you now have access to large areas of open land. You can of course continue to use rights of way footpaths to cross this land, but the main difference is that you can now lawfully leave the path and wander at will, but only in areas designated as access land.

Where to Walk

Areas now covered by the new access rights – Access Land – are shown on

Ordnance Survey Explorer maps bearing the access land symbol on the front cover.

'Access Land' is shown on Ordnance Survey maps by a light yellow tint surrounded by a pale orange border. New orange coloured 'i' symbols on the maps will show the location of permanent access information boards installed by the access authorities.

Restrictions

The right to walk on access land may lawfully be restricted by landowners. Landowners can, for any reason, restrict access for up to 28 days in any year. They cannot however close the land:

- on bank holidays;
- for more than four Saturdays and Sundays in a year;

- on any Saturday from 1 June to 11 August; or
- on any Sunday from 1 June to the end of September.

They have to provide local authorities with five working days' notice before the date of closure unless the land involved is an area of less than five hectares or the closure is for less than four hours. In these cases land-owners only need to provide two hours' notice.

Whatever restrictions are put into place on access land they have no effect on existing rights of way, and you can continue to walk on them.

Dogs

Dogs can be taken on access land, but must be kept on leads of two metres or less between 1 March and 31 July, and at all times where they are near livestock. In addition landowners may impose a ban on all dogs from fields where lambing takes place for up to six weeks in any year. Dogs may be banned from moorland used for grouse shooting and breeding for up to five years.

In the main, walkers following the routes in this book will continue to follow existing rights of way, but a knowledge and understanding of the law as it affects walkers, plus the ability to distinguish access land marked on the maps, will enable anyone who wishes to depart from paths that cross access land either to take a shortcut, to enjoy a view or to explore.

General Obstructions

Obstructions can sometimes cause a problem on a walk and the most common of these is where the path across a field has been ploughed over. It is legal for a farmer to plough up a path provided that it is restored within two weeks. This does not always happen and you are faced with the dilemma of following the line of the path, even if this means treading on crops, or walking round the edge of the field. Although the later course of action seems the most sensible, it does mean that you would be trespassing.

Other obstructions can vary from overhanging vegetation to wire fences across the path, locked gates or even a cattle feeder on the path.

Use common sense. If you can get round the obstruction without causing damage, do so. Otherwise only remove as much of the obstruction as is necessary to secure passage.

If the right of way is blocked and cannot be followed, there is a long-standing view that in such circumstances there is a right to deviate, but this cannot wholly be relied on. Although it is accepted in law that highways (and that includes rights of way) are for the public service, and if the usual track is impassable, it is for the general good that people should be entitled to pass into another line. However, this should not be taken as indicating a right to deviate whenever a way becomes impassable. If in doubt, retreat.

Report obstructions to the local authority and/or the Ramblers' Association.

 Useful Organisations

Beatrix Potter Gallery
Main Street, Hawkshead, Cumbria, LA22 0NS
Open from mid-February–end of October
Times and admission prices vary
Tel. 015394 36355
www.nationaltrust.org.uk

Cumbria Tourist Board
Ashleigh, Holly Road, Bowness-on-Windermere, Cumbria LA23 2AQ
Tel. 015394 44444
www.golakes.co.uk

Dove Cottage
Located on the A591
Open daily (except Christmas and January) from 09.30–17.30 (fee)
Tel. 015394 35544
www.wordsworth.org.uk

Friends of the Lake District
Murley Moss, Oxenholme Road, Kendal, Cumbria LA9 7SS
Tel. 01539 720788
www.fld.org.uk

Lake District National Park Authority information centres *(*not open all year)*:
*Ambleside: 015394 32729
*Bowness Bay: 015394 42895
*Broughton-in-Furness: 01229 716115
*Coniston: 015394 41533
*Glenridding: 017684 82414
*Grasmere: 015394 35245
*Hawkshead: 015394 36525
Keswick: 017687 72645
*Pooley Bridge: 017684 86530
*Waterhead: 015394 32729

Lake District National Park Visitor Centre
Brockhole, Windermere, Cumbria LA23 1LJ
Tel. 015394 46601
www.lake-district.gov.uk

Long Distance Walkers' Association
www.ldwa.org.uk

National Trust
Central Regional Office:
The Hollens, Grasmere, Ambleside,
Cumbria LA22 9QZ
Tel. 08706 095391
www.nationaltrust.org.uk

Ordnance Survey
Romsey Road, Maybush,
Southampton SO16 4GU
Tel. 08456 05 05 05 (Lo-call)
www.ordnancesurvey.co.uk

Ramblers' Association
2nd Floor, Camelford House, 87–90
Albert Embankment, London SE1 7TW
Tel. 020 7339 8500
www.ramblers.org.uk

Rydal Mount
Rydal, Nr. Ambleside, Cumbria, LA22 9LU
Open daily from March–October,
9.30–17.00 (in winter from Wednesday–
Sunday, 11.00–16.00 (except Christmas
period) (fee)
Tel. 015394 33002
www.rydalmount.co.uk

Townend
Troutbeck, Windermere, Cumbria, LA23 1LB
Open from March–September from

11.00–15.00 in March and then 17.00
(unless poor light invokes an earlier
closing time) Tel: 015394 32628
www.nationaltrust.org.uk

Youth Hostels Association
Trevelyan House, Dimple Road,
Matlock, Derbyshire DE4 3YH
Tel. 01629 592600
www.yha.org.uk

Ordnance Survey maps of the Lake District

The Lake District is covered by Ordnance Survey 1:50 000 (1$\frac{1}{4}$ inches to 1 mile or 2cm to 1km) scale Landranger map sheets 85, 86, 89, 90, 91, 96, 97 and 98. These all-purpose maps are packed with information to help you explore the area. Viewpoints, picnic sites, places of interest and caravan and camping sites are shown, as well as public rights of way information such as footpaths and bridleways.

To examine the Lake District in more detail, and especially if you are planning walks, Ordnance Survey Explorer maps at 1:25 000 (2$\frac{1}{2}$ inches to 1 mile or 4cm to 1km) scale are ideal. Four such maps cover the main Lake District National Park:

OL4 (The English Lakes –
    North-western area)
OL5 (The English Lakes –
    North-eastern area)
OL6 (The English Lakes –
    South-western area)
OL7 (The English Lakes –
    South-eastern area)

The Lake District area is also covered by Ordnance Survey touring map number 3, at 1 inch to 1$\frac{1}{2}$ miles or 1cm to 1km (1:100 000) scale, which includes useful guide information on the reverse.

To get to the Lake District, use the Ordnance Survey Travel Map-Route at 1:625 000 (1 inch to 10 miles or 4cm to 25km) scale or OS Travel Map-Road 4 (Northern England) at 1:250 000 (1 inch to 4 miles or 1cm to 2.5km) scale.

Ordnance Survey maps and guides are available from most booksellers, stationers and newsagents.

Further Information